Living a Successful Christian Life

Matthew 6:33 says, "Seek the Kingdom of God above all else, and live righteously, and He will give you everything you need." (NLT)

Flora O. Erome-Utunedi

2/15/15

ISBN: 1502319187

ISBN 13: 9781502319180

Contents

Foreword

My wife, Andrea, and I have known Flora for a number of years. She is a woman of prayer, has a discerning spirit, and is passionate about the truth in the Word of God. Flora's passion for the Word of God is evident in this book. She has done a great job of researching scripture to find those truths that set people free to live the life God has created them for.

Everyone wants to have success in life. This book gives a great spiritual foundation for how to find and live out that success. Success has been defined in many ways, but the true measure of success will be when we stand face-to-face with God, and we hear those words all Christians want to hear: "His lord said unto him, Well done, good and faithful servant; thou hast been faithful over a few things, I will make you ruler over many things: enter thou into the joy of thy lord" (Matthew 25:23 KJV). This book will give you some keys to help you unlock the potential you have in Jesus. It is a tremendous resource for successful living packed with scripture to inspire positive steps in life. Let this book be something that helps you find success through Jesus.

I recommend you read this book and discover the truth God has in store for your life. Flora has taken key words that all of us identify with and has applied scriptural truth to help us unlock success in life and to live the life God has planned for us.

Rev. Mark Williams, lead pastor Beddington Pentecostal Church

Sister Flora has touched a vital area in Christianity that the Church needs today more than other generations past. The Gospel seems unattractive to unbelievers because they cannot see the distinct features that separate a believer from the others. God is no respecter of persons. "Then Peter opened his mouth, and said, Of a truth I perceive that God is no respecter of persons..." (Acts 10: 34 KJV). For the Church to receive power like the time of old, we need to return to the God of power. Since He is Holy, and His eyes are too pure to behold iniquity—"thou art of purer eyes to behold evil, and canst not look on iniquity: wherefore lookest thou upon them that deal treacherously, and holdest thy tongue when the wicked devoureth the man that is more righteous than he?" (Habakkuk 1:13)—we need to cleanse our garment and walk in purity and transparency. Then the power will fall, and sinners will desire to know the same Jesus who washed us clean and spotless. I recommend this book to anyone who desires to know more of God and how to walk with Him in this world and who will, in the life to come, enjoy eternal life.

Pastor Samuel Eleko
Redemption Bible Church, Calgary

Acknowledgments

My deepest appreciation to Almighty God, our Lord and Savior, Jesus Christ, and the Holy Spirit for the opportunity of knowing Him and the ability He has given to me to write this book to His honor. I thank God for using me as a vessel to communicate this message, and I thank Him for His grace. This book is dedicated to God the Father, almighty.

I pledge my total allegiance to the Word of God; the Word of God is the Word of Life. Let it be a lamp unto my feet and a light unto my path. God, help me to hide Your Word in my heart so that I may not sin against You. So help me God, amen.

I am also indebted to my dear husband/engineer/deacon, Erome Utunedi, and to our beloved children—Jesse, John, Joshua, Jeremiah, and Jefferson—for their wonderful support on this project.

I would like to give a special thanks to my pastor, Mark Williams, of Beddington Pentecostal Church (Calgary) for his prayers, contributions, and encouragement—and also a thanks to the rest of the pastors in the church for their encouragement. Thank you, women in the prayer ministry, for your prayers and encouragement and to everyone else who supported me in that regard. A special thanks also goes out to pastor Samuel Eleko, of Redemption Bible Church (Calgary), for his contributions and his support and a thank-you to brother Marvin Persaud and family, and sister C. Kerr as well, of Calgary Full Gospel Church (Calgary), for their help. I appreciate you all. God richly bless you, in Jesus's name.

My appreciation also goes to the team of CreateSpace publishing company for their help in making this book a success.

Summary

This book is all about the revelation that God gave to me in a dream to the Church. The message is how the Church, the body of Christ, should live a successful Christian life. God is telling the Church today that to live a successful Christian life, the body of Christ must run away from evil and embrace holiness and righteousness in a personal walk with Him. The Church is encouraged to go back to the basics, which is the Word of God, and to be Christ followers who practice His Word. The Word of God is the foundation of Christianity. Where the Church has lost it, God is calling His Church for true repentance to receive His forgiveness because He is willing to forgive His Church. The Church today needs to hear messages from the pulpit about holiness and righteousness to draw near to God and to experience His power.

The introductory chapter attempts to define success and being successful as viewed by the secular world and as explained by the Holy Bible, the Word of God. The secular world has a view of what success is all about. More often than not in the world's view, the definition of success leads to a meaningless life. Success as explained by the Word of God in the Holy Bible and revealed to the world by our Lord and Savior Jesus Christ, leads to a meaningful, successful life.

The concept of living a successful Christian life, as revealed by the Word of God, is discussed here. Ample scriptural keys to living a successful Christian life are also explored.

The book also deals with examples of people who successfully worked with God in the Holy Bible. It is clear that Christians have no excuse not to follow the precepts ordered by God and further expounded on by Jesus Christ. It is possible to work with God and be successful, by His grace. Combining the scriptural keys and the examples of those who successfully worked with God should provide us with the needed impetus to live a successful Christian Life.

Critical success factors in addition to the above are further discussed in this book. These are fearing the Lord God Almighty, knowing the Lord Jesus Christ, and honoring your father and mother. "The fear of the Lord is the beginning of wisdom; a good understanding have all they that do his commandments: his praise endureth forever." (Psalms 111:10 KJV) Divine Understanding and Wisdom comes from the power that is in the Word of God. To know Jesus Christ is the key to success and through Him the Church is made righteous. To live a long and satisfying life we must honor our fathers and mothers!

My prayers are for you to read and meditate on this book, but keep in mind that the Holy Bible must always remain the primary guide of the Church. And by using this guide, I have no doubt that not only will you experience visible changes in your walk with Christ, it will also ultimately lead you to become a successful Christian by His grace.

"Let us hear the conclusion of the whole matter: Fear God, and keep His commandments: for this is the whole duty of man. For God shall bring every work into judgment, with every secret thing, whether it be good, or whether it be evil" (Ecclesiastes 12:13 KJV).

To live a successful Christian life is challenging, but it is possible by His grace. When a Christian takes the right decision to live for God, he or she realizes that there is no better life outside following Jesus Christ. Let us not be fooled by the glamour and the illusions of wealth, fame, and self-righteousness or be religious without the power of God. Now is the time to decide to follow God; the alternative will lead to nowhere—a life in cycles. "And now my dear brothers and sisters one final thing; fix your thoughts on what is true and honorable, and right and pure, and lovely and admirable. Think about things that are excellent and worthy of praise" (Philippians 4:8 NLT). I sincerely pray for you and all reading this book that God, in His infinite mercies, will grant you the grace to live a successful Christian life, by the power of Holy Spirit. Amen.

Introduction

Agnes M, Guralnik DB, *Webster's New World College Dictionary.* Fourth Edition. Cleveland: Wiley Publishing, Inc., 2004.

Suc•cess (sək ses') n. 1 [Obs.] result, outcome 2 a) a favorable or satisfactory outcome or result b) something having such an outcome 3 the gaining of wealth, fame, rank, etc. 4 a successful person ("success," def. 1–4).

Suc•cess•ful (-fəl) adj. 1 coming about, taking place, or turning out to be as was hoped for *[a successful mission]* 2 having achieved success; specifically having gained wealth, fame, etc. ("successful," def. 1–2).

What is defined as success or successful? One leads to the other. The secular world views success as the attainment of wealth, favor/eminence, or a favorable/desired outcome. Successful can mean resulting/terminating in success or gaining/having gained success; however, defining success or successful in the absence of the influence of God leads to a meaningless life.

First Chronicles 22:13 says, "For you will be successful if you carefully obey the decrees and regulations the Lord gave to Israel through Moses. Be strong and courageous; do not be afraid or lose heart!" (NLT, emphasis added).

This instruction above was given to Solomon by King David, his father. It also applies to the Church today. The key word in this passage is obedience to the Word of God. The outcome of obedience to the Word of God tells the Church that the individual will be successful. Obedience to the Word of God drives away fear and makes the Christian courageous to speak the truth without compromise. The Word of God brings orderliness and fulfillment in the life of a Christian. Lasting success can only be achieved from the incorruptible and undefiled Word of God.

Therefore, success—according to the Bible—is about obedience to the Word of God and living a Christlike life. Wealth, favor/eminence, or a favorable/desired outcome are by-products of this Christlike life. Matthew 6:33 says, "Seek the Kingdom of God above all else, and live righteously, and He will give you everything you need" (NLT).

Success comes as a result of obedience to God. Christians will live a successful life when their top priority is the acquisition of the Kingdom of God, which can only be done by surrendering their hearts and doing the will of God. Obedience to the Word of God shows the degree of love that a Christian has for God.

Love and obedience are the key ingredients to becoming successful as followers of Christ, as the Holy Bible reveals to us.

Second Timothy 3:16 says, "All Scripture is inspired by God and is useful to teach us what is true and to make us realize what is wrong in our lives. It corrects us when we are wrong and teaches us to do what is right" (NLT). The love of God is holy, pure, and genuine, and it never fails; it conquers because the love of God is powerful. The Bible says, hope, faith, and love, but the greatest is love.

Luke 10:27–28 says, "He answered, '"Love the Lord your God with all your heart and with all your soul and with all your strength and with all your mind"; and, "Love your neighbor as yourself."' 'You have answered correctly,' Jesus replied. 'Do this and you will live'" (NIV). In other words, do this, and you will live—successfully.

First Corinthians 13:1–8 says,

> If I speak in the tongues of men or of angels, but do not have love, I am only a resounding gong or a clanging cymbal. If I have the gift of prophecy and can fathom all mysteries and all knowledge, and if I have a faith that can move mountains, but do not have love, I am nothing. If

> I give all I possess to the poor and give over my body to hardship that I may boast, but do not have love, I gain nothing. Love is patient, love is kind. It does not envy, it does not boast, it is not proud. It does not dishonor others, it is not self-seeking, it is not easily angered, it keeps no record of wrongs. Love does not delight in evil but rejoices with the truth. It always protects, always trusts, always hopes, and always perseveres. Love never fails. But where there are prophecies, they will cease; where there are tongues, they will be stilled; where there is knowledge, it will pass away (NIV).

There is no better formula to work successfully with God than this.

Obedience to the Word of God brings blessing and gives a fulfilled life. God's desire for the Church as a corporate body is to be an assembly of people of integrity. According to the Holy Bible, the presence of God left King Saul because of his disobedience to the instructions of God. First Samuel 28:15 says, "Why have you disturbed me by calling me back?" Samuel asked Saul. "I am in deep trouble," Saul replied, "The Philistines are at war with me, and God has left me and won't reply by prophets or dreams, So I have called for you to tell me what to do" (NLT). Living a successful Christian life is living for God. The right door to God the Father is going through Jesus Christ. Jesus said in John 14:6, "I am the way, the truth, and the life. No one can come to the Father except through me" (NLT).

The Holy Bible is the unique, flawless, authoritative, and God-inspired Word. These words of God are dependable, trustworthy, and reliable. The Word of God is the mirror the Christian looks at daily to form godly character and live a successful Christian life. Job 1:1 says, "There once was a man named Job who lived in the land of Uz. He was blameless—a man of complete integrity. He feared God and stayed away from evil" (NLT). By all accounts, Job lived a successful life despite his challenges.

James 3:13 says, "If you are wise and understand God's ways, prove it by living an honorable life, doing good works with the humility that comes from wisdom" (NLT).

The foundation of a successful Christian life is built on teachings, life, death, and the resurrection of our Lord Jesus Christ. The truth is that God wants the Church, His children, to be transparent in everything. Living a successful Christian life comes only for the hearers and doers of the Word of God. In Luke 8:21, Jesus said, "My mother and brothers are those who hear God's word and put it into practice" (NIV).

God want His children to live righteous lives for His glory as His children of the kingdom and not to live for themselves. Without sacrifice a Christian cannot live a successful Christian life. What is the Lord telling you today to sacrifice because of His sake? The members of the Church, as a body of Christ, are Christ's ambassadors. The question that readily comes to mind is, is the Church still operating in that first love when it says, "Yes, Lord, I will follow You"? What are you using the gift He has given to you for? Or is there anything else that is lord over your life? God's intention is to grant our hearts' desires according to His purpose when we do the right thing first by living out the Word. According to the Holy Bible, no one can serve two masters. The Christian who desires to be successful treasures the Word of God in his or her heart. Matthew 6:19–33 says,

> Do not store up for yourselves treasures on earth, where moths and vermin destroy, and where thieves break in and steal. But store up for yourselves treasures in heaven, where moths and vermin do not destroy, and where thieves do not break in and steal. For where your treasure is, there your heart will be also. The eye is the lamp of the body. If your eyes are healthy, your whole body will be full of light. But if your eyes are unhealthy, your whole body will be full of darkness. If then the light within you is darkness, how great is that darkness! No one can serve two masters. Either you will hate the one and love the

> other, or you will be devoted to the one and despise the other. You cannot serve both God and money. Therefore I tell you, do not worry about your life, what you will eat or drink; or about your body, what you will wear. Is not life more than food, and the body more than clothes? Look at the birds of the air; they do not sow or reap or store away in barns, and yet your heavenly Father feeds them. Are you not much more valuable than they? Can any one of you by worrying add a single hour to your life? And why do you worry about clothes? See how the flowers of the field grow. They do not labor or spin. Yet I tell you that not even Solomon in all his splendor was dressed like one of these. If that is how God clothes the grass of the field, which is here today and tomorrow is thrown into the fire, will He not much more clothe you—you of little faith? So do not worry, saying, "What shall we eat?" or "What shall we drink?" or "What shall we wear?" For the pagans run after all these things, and your heavenly Father knows that you need them. *But seek first His kingdom and His righteousness, and all these things will be given to you as well* (NIV, emphasis added).

The Church is admonished in this passage that "cares and worries of this world" will do a Christian no good but rather create unnecessary anxiety. The Church should learn how to trust God completely for daily needs. This is not a call to idleness but a call to engage in diligent endeavors with God at the center of it. The fear of the unknown has made some Christians depend on their ability to get rich or try to get things done in an ungodly manner. The result is that they become unnecessarily anxious and commit acts that should not be associated with a Christian. It has even deprived some Christians of their joy because their loyalty is divided between God and money. Please repent and learn how to trust God completely to provide so that you will live a successful Christian life. Every need will be taken care of by God when the Church chooses to walk with Him uprightly. A

Christian should not be anxious for anything but rather make your request known to God in prayer. Worry can actually rob a Christian of peace and also of the valuable time that he or she is supposed to pray to God or read the Holy Bible or engage in a fruitful endeavor.

On May 16, 2013, God gave me a revelation on how to become and remain a successful Christian. In the dream, I was called upon to preach the Word to a large audience. As I was about to speak, God led me to preach about living a successful Christian life. God used me as a vessel to proclaim His Word. It was a clear revelation. When I woke up, I wrote what He had led me to say, and I began to meditate on the words. It was clear to me that God was telling His Church something, because the message is in accordance with His Word.

Christians should wake up and return to the Lord where a wrong path has been followed. Now is the time for a spiritual awakening. The message is that Christians can live successful Christian lives by His grace. According to the saying of our Lord and Savior, Jesus Christ, "He that hath ears to hear, let him hear. (Matthew 11:15 KJV)." It is human nature to want to be successful in one's chosen career. Though the individual feels a sense of achievement, the associated success is incomplete until that individual totally surrenders his or her life to Jesus Christ. Success in a career or goal we have set down for ourselves can be only temporary without Jesus Christ.

Psalm 127:1 says, "Unless the Lord builds the house, the builders labor in vain. Unless the Lord watches over the city, the guards stand watch in vain" (NIV). Who is the builder of your entire life as a Christian? I have no doubt in my heart that Almighty God wants His Church as a body to be cleansed, to be successful, and to fight the good fight of faith until believers will meet Him face-to-face. Then He will tell us, "Well done, my faithful servants." The Church is reminded again that heavenly inheritance awaits Christians who endure to the end in obedience in their walk with God. That will be the complete success by His grace. He led me to say that the Church as an assembly of His people should, first, *fear the Lord God Almighty;* second, *should know the Lord Jesus Christ*; and third, *should honor their parents.* I was called upon to deliver this message (in the revelation God gave to me) to the Church as the body of Christ.

Living a successful Christian life is very challenging, both spiritually and physically. The Christian lives by the Word of God daily to improve and add value to his or her life. Christians acknowledge that the knowledge of God and the Word of God are total, supreme, and necessary requirements to grow to become Christlike. The knowledge of God stands forever. To be successful as a Christian covers every aspect of life—spiritual, emotional, physical, and environmental.

Doing the will of God is the center of the message of Jesus Christ. Becoming a successful Christian and having a relationship with God have to be genuine and based on the Word of God. Any relationship built on lies is already faulty, but a relationship built on the Word of God stands. Anyone who builds on a faulty foundation is not of Christ. Matthew 7:24–27 says,

> Therefore everyone who hears these words of mine and puts them into practice is like a wise man who built his house on the rock. The rain came down, the streams rose, and the winds blew and beat against that house; yet it did not fall, because it had its foundation on the rock. But everyone who hears these words of mine and does not put them into practice is like a foolish man who built his house on sand. The rain came down, the streams rose, and the winds blew and beat against that house, and it fell with a great crash (NIV).

Obedience to the Word of God builds the right foundation for a true success. God's Word gives complete knowledge and truth to a successful living, when God's Word takes priority in the life of a Christian.

First Kings 2:3 says, "Observe the requirements of the Lord your God, and follow all His ways. Keep the decrees, commands, regulations, and laws written in the Law of Moses so that you will be successful in all you do and wherever you go" (NLT).

When a Christian keeps close the Word of God into his or her heart and follows the ways of God, the result is that the Christian will be successful in all he or she does, wherever that person goes. There is no limit for God's blessings when the Church walks with God in obedience.

1. Living a Successful Christian Life

1.1 Introduction

Becoming a successful Christian is a continuous and progressive walk with God. The Bible says, "Come close to God and God will come close to you. Wash your hands, you sinners; purify your hearts, for your loyalty is divided between God and the world" (James 4:8 NLT). A Christian needs a close relationship with God for spiritual growth. It takes the special grace of God and the willingness of the Christian to walk with Him in obedience. This is where the grace of God has a role to play—when Christians allow God to be in full control of their lives. It is by His grace, lest any man should boast. Grace means God's free and unmerited favor and mercy toward sinful humanity. Becoming a successful Christian is a tough road to walk, but thanks be to God who has given everything it takes for Church members to live successful Christian lives. God's Word has pointed Christianity in the direction to follow.

Matthew 7:13–14 says, "Enter through the narrow gate. For wide is the gate and broad is the road that leads to destruction, and many enter through it. But small is the gate and narrow the road that leads to life and only a few find it" (NIV).

Hallelujah, for those who endure to the end will have their reward. Jesus Christ has empowered Christians to live their lives to the fullest by the power of the Holy Spirit, so the Church can be successful. John 10:1–10 says,

> "Very truly I tell you Pharisees, anyone who does not enter the sheep pen by the gate, but climbs in by some other way, is a thief and a robber. The one who enters by the gate is the shepherd of the sheep. The gatekeeper opens the gate for him, and the sheep listen to his voice. He calls his own sheep by name and leads them out. When he has brought out all his own, he goes on ahead of them, and his sheep follow him because they know his voice. But they will never follow a stranger; in fact, they will run away from him because they do not recognize a stranger's voice." Jesus used this figure of speech, but the Pharisees did not understand what He was telling them. Therefore Jesus said again, "Very truly I tell you, I am the gate for the sheep. All who have come before me are thieves and robbers, but the sheep have not listened to them. I am the gate; whoever enters through me will be saved. They will come in and go out, and find pasture. The thief comes only to steal and kill and destroy; I have come that they may have life, and have it to the full" (NIV).

Following the exemplary leadership of Jesus Christ is the key to having a successful Christian life.

Christians have to let go of some of the baggage they had before knowing Jesus Christ. Hebrews 12:1–2 says, "Therefore, since we are surrounded by such a great cloud of witnesses, let us throw off everything that hinders and the sin that so easily entangles. And let us run with perseverance the race marked out for us, fixing our eyes on Jesus, the pioneer and perfecter of faith. For the joy set before Him He endured the cross, scorning its shame, and sat down at the right hand of the throne of God" (NIV). Christ endured the pain because of the sins of humanity.

The only way to appreciate God for what He has done is to trust and obey Him. Is there any specific thing God is telling you as a Christian to surrender for His sake, something you are struggling with? For you to be successful in the Christian walk, you have to consciously and willingly denounce that particular thing

God has been telling you to forsake because of His kingdom. Pleasing God and not man should be the goal of the Church, no matter the position you are in as a Christian. The outward appearance should reflect what is inside. The good news is that God sees the heart and the motives behind every step.

The only tradition that will make a Christian successful is having a true knowledge of the Word of God. The Word of God is the tradition of the Church. Adopting the leadership example of Jesus Christ will make the Church more effective and productive, because Jesus Christ is the standard of the Church. The life of anyone who encounters Jesus Christ will change forever. This change is real, because the apostle Paul and others in the Word of God experienced it.

The same power of Jesus Christ that changed the apostle Paul's life is still very much active and powerful today. True repentance brings a change of heart to be pure. "Blessed are the pure in heart, for they will see God" (Matthew 5:8 NIV). It is the grace of God that turns the Christian from sin. Romans 6:1–4 says, "What shall we say, then? Shall we go on sinning so that grace may increase? By no means! We are those who have died to sin; how can we live in it any longer? Or don't you know that all of us who were baptized into Christ Jesus were baptized into His death? We were therefore buried with Him through baptism into death in order that, just as Christ was raised from the dead through the glory of the Father, we too may live a new life" (NIV).

The grace of God is sufficient to see us through if the Church is willing to walk with Him. Titus 2:11–12 says, "For the grace of God has been revealed, bringing salvation to all people. And we are instructed to turn from godless living and sinful pleasures. We should live in this evil world with wisdom, righteousness, and devotion to God" (NLT).

Don't struggle with sin. Confess it to Jesus, and repent from it; you will see how amazingly successful your walk with God will be. Christians shouldn't allow sin to rob us of our salvation. The success of the Church is in Jesus Christ alone. Without Jesus Christ there is no success; that is why the Church shouldn't drift away from His presence. Christians react to the leading of the power of the Holy Spirit. They should have the mind-set of Jesus Christ. Their hearts have to be equipped and occupied with the Word of God (Jesus Christ is the Word), from which Christians draw nutrients daily. They have to be in the Word of God, and the Word should be in them. Accepting the Lord Jesus Christ and obeying the Word of God—that is Christianity. Living a successful Christian life involves complete surrender to Almighty God. Christians delight in the things that matters to God. Jeremiah 9:23–24 says,

> "Let not the wise boast of their wisdom
> or the strong boast of their strength
> or the rich boast of their riches,
> but let the one who boasts boast about this:
> that they have the understanding to know me,
> that I am the Lord, who exercises kindness,
> justice and righteousness on earth,
> for in these I delight,"
> declares the Lord (NIV).

The Church should boast only in the name of the Lord, because through Him we can do all things. Christians need to rely on the power of the Lord Jesus Christ and to trust His Word completely and Him alone. Prayer is very essential in the lives of Christians. Two pillars of a successful Christian are (1) to know and live out the Word of God and (2) to pray without ceasing. Ephesians 3:14–20 says,

> For this reason I kneel before the Father, from whom every family in heaven and on earth derives its name. I pray that out of His glorious riches He may strengthen you with power through His Spirit in your inner being, so that Christ may dwell in your hearts through faith. And I pray that you, being rooted and established in love, may have power, together with all the Lord's holy people, to

> grasp how wide and long and high and deep is the love of Christ, and to know this love that surpasses knowledge—that you may be filled to the measure of all the fullness of God. Now to Him who is able to do immeasurably more than all we ask or imagine, according to His power that is at work within us... (NIV).

Without studying the Word of God—which is the authority of Christians—and prayers, living a successful Christian life will be very difficult. The Word of God gives the Church an understanding of who God is and knowledge of His heart. The Christian who knows the biblical principles of prayer takes every matter, both big and small, to God in prayer. Matthew 7:7–11 says,

> Ask and it will be given to you; seek and you will find; knock and the door will be opened to you. For everyone who asks receives; the one who seeks finds; and to the one who knocks, the door will be opened. Which of you, if your son asks for bread, will give him a stone? Or if he asks for a fish, will give him a snake? If you, then, though you are evil, know how to give good gifts to your children, how much more will your Father in heaven give good gifts to those who ask him! (NIV)

When members of the Church take their needs to God according to His will, the results will be answered prayers. The committed Christ follower seeks the approval of God in everything he or she embarks on. Christians know things cannot go wrong when God is involved—and most importantly, when He approves of them.

Romans 8:28 says, "And we know that in all things God works for the good of those who love Him, who have been called according to His purpose" (NIV). Even when a situation already committed into the hands of God wants to go in a direction not ordained by Him, He will step in and correct it. If the Enemy intends it for evil, God will turn it around for good. God is all sufficient. He is the solution to any kind of problem. Satisfaction is in Christ alone.

The drive among Christians for wealth, power, fame, and position has made some sell their birthrights. The undue craving for miracles has made a lot of people who confess Jesus Christ as their Lord and personal Savior stain their hands, or they have turned away from the truth. Are you in that category? The Lord is saying, denounce it, and come back to Him. Mark 16:16–18 says, "Whoever believes and is baptized will be saved, but whoever does not believe will be condemned. And these signs will accompany those who believe: In My name they will drive out demons; they will speak in new tongues; they will pick up snakes with their hands; and when they drink deadly poison, it will not hurt them at all; they will place their hands on sick people, and they will get well" (NIV) Divine miracles come only from the power that is in the Word of God. The Church should hold on to the promises of God, because the believers know God is very faithful to His Word. What God says, He will do. He will not withhold any good thing from His children. Have you waited too long and gone your own way through perverted means to have it? God is telling you to come back to Him and repent. Second Chronicles 7:14 says, "If my people, who are called by my name, will humble themselves and pray and seek my face and turn from their wicked ways, then I will hear from heaven, and I will forgive their sin and will heal their land" (NIV).

A Christian who craves to be successful runs away from evil. He knows God detests evil. That is why Jesus Christ came to destroy the works of the devil. He did the finished work on the cross with His blood, death, and His resurrection. Whosoever believes in Him will be saved and will do the work of the Father, because He lives inside anyone who believes in the work Christ has done.

When an individual truly repents and abides in His secret place, the Christian will be successful. Repentance has to be a complete change from the heart in order to experience success. The success the Word of God teaches the Church is based not on materialism but on growing in God's wisdom and knowledge of His Word, filled with the power of the Holy Spirit and the power of His might to do His will. When a believer prays, sings, or preaches, heaven responds, and the kingdom of darkness is in trouble. When the believer mounts the pulpit to proclaim the Word of God, the devil and his agents tremble and become very angry, because the devil cannot stand the Word of God. Christians know that they operate in and with the power of God. "Ye are of God, little children, and have overcome them: because greater is he that is in you, than he that is in the world." (First John 4:4 KJV) Committed Christians know the power of God that operates in them because they walk in obedience with God. Total obedience plays a very important role in walking with God. First Samuel 15:22 says, "But Samuel replied, 'What is more pleasing to the Lord; your burnt offerings and sacrifices or your obedience to His voice? Listen! Obedience is better than sacrifice, and submission is better than offering the fat of rams'" (NLT).

1.2 Scriptural Keys to Success

Successful Christians are redeemed believers who have completely surrendered to the lordship of God. Their spiritual journey is with God, and by His grace He helps the believers live as successful Christians.

Each letter in "Successful Christian" has been identified below, accompanied by major pillars of Christian living that lead to becoming a successful Christian. Believers led by the Spirit of God know God has designed His Church to be united. God's desire is that we would dwell in unity as the body of Christ. By God's grace we confidently know God will hear us when we call upon Him. Christians should always live thankful lives, especially for the salvation received through Christ. That is why the Church must exalt God in songs/praises and prayers for the salvation He has freely offered to everyone. The salvation of the Christian is secured in Jesus Christ alone, because in Him is the true foundation of success. The Christian knows that the precious blood of Jesus Christ and the forgiveness of our sins bought and redeemed believers. God requires from us only obedience to walk with Him with sincere hearts and a genuine repentance.

1.2.1 Spirit

Jesus, filled with the Holy Spirit, said, "It is written, 'The Spirit of the Lord is upon me, because He hath anointed Me to preach the gospel to the poor; He hath sent Me to heal the broken hearted, to preach deliverance to the captives, and recovering of sight to the blind, to set at liberty them that are bruised'" (Luke 4:18 KJV).

The words of Jesus Christ tell the Church that without the power of the Holy Spirit, a Christian cannot function and will not be spiritually successful. To live a successful Christian life, you must have, and be filled with, the Holy Spirit by asking God Almighty for the gift of the Holy Spirit through prayers. The anointing in the power of the Holy Spirit in the lives of Christians is very important to do the work of God. The Holy Spirit is the number-one priority for the Church to live a successful Christian life after receiving Christ as Lord and personal Savior. Ephesians 1:13 says, "And you also were included in Christ when you heard the message of truth, the gospel of your salvation. When you believed, you were marked in Him with a seal, the promised Holy Spirit" (NIV)." The Spirit is God's guarantee that He will give us the inheritance He promised and that He has purchased us to be His own people. He did this so we would praise and glorify Him". (Ephesians 1:14 NLT)

The Spirit of God is the seal that plays an important role in the life of Christ followers so they can be successful. God baptized the Christian with the Holy Spirit and with various gifts in the body of Christ to enable the Church to live out the Word and do the work of God. First Corinthians 12:1–13 says,

> Now about the gifts of the Spirit, brothers and sisters, I do not want you to be uninformed. You know that when you were pagans, somehow or other you were influenced and led astray to mute idols. Therefore I want you to know that

> no one who is speaking by the Spirit of God says, "Jesus be cursed," and no one can say, "Jesus is Lord," except by the Holy Spirit. There are different kinds of gifts, but the same Spirit distributes them. There are different kinds of service, but the same Lord. There are different kinds of working, but in all of them and in everyone it is the same God at work. Now to each one the manifestation of the Spirit is given for the common good. To one there is given through the Spirit a message of wisdom, to another a message of knowledge by means of the same Spirit, to another faith by the same Spirit, to another gifts of healing by that one Spirit, to another miraculous powers, to another prophecy, to another distinguishing between spirits, to another speaking in different kinds of tongues, and to still another the interpretation of tongues. All these are the work of one and the same Spirit, and He distributes them to each one, just as He determines. Just as a body, though one, has many parts, but all its many parts form one body, so it is with Christ. For we were all baptized by one Spirit so as to form one body—whether Jews or Gentiles, slave or free—and we were all given the one Spirit to drink (NIV).

Redeemed Christians hear from God, and every one of their steps is ordered through the power of the Holy Spirit. Christians are true followers and worshippers of Jesus Christ. The power of God controls them. Which spirit are you subject to, and which is controlling you? The Holy Spirit teaches, directs, and counsels Christians to be successful in their various callings. According to the Bible, "For those who are led by the spirit of God are the children of God" (Romans 8:14 NIV).

1.2.2 Unity

John 17:23 says, "I am in them and you are in me. May they experience such perfect unity that the world will know that you sent me and that you love them as much as you love me" (NLT).

Ephesians 2:13 says, "But now you have been united in Christ Jesus. Once you were far away from God, but now you have been brought near to Him through the blood of Christ" (NLT).

Proclaiming the unity of God and dwelling in peace and unity are critical steps toward becoming a successful Christian. This success is bound in the true love of God that has been freely given to humanity. The believer is expected to be an agent of this love of Christ and bring unity to the Church. The Bible says these three will last forever—faith, hope, and love—and the greatest of these is love. First Corinthians 13:13 says, "God is the author not of confusion but of peace" (NLT). All churches that are founded on the solid name of Jesus Christ are one, as the body of Christ.

The love of God brought unity to the Church through Christ. Unity brings peace and harmony. The Church should live united, and it is possible by His grace to live peaceably with all men. Doing so can be difficult without the help of God, but with God it is possible. The Bible admonishes the Church to live in harmony with one another. Love one another; that is the will of God for the Church, and this love is required to successfully run the race. The atmosphere of the kingdom of God is love; that is why the unity has to start here on earth because to love is the will of God. The Bible says, "May your kingdom come soon. May your Will be done on earth, as it is in Heaven" (Mathew 6:10 NLT).

1.2.3 Christ

He is the Savior, the Redeemer of the world, the only access to God the Father. Christ is no more in the grave; He is risen and alive. The Church should bear in mind that Christ is coming soon. Until He comes, the Church has to do the work of Father God through Jesus Christ. God has set a day for judging the world with justice through Jesus Christ, whom God appointed by raising Him from the dead. Christ is the Head of the Church. He is the author and finisher of our faith; that is why everything has to be done through Him. The joy of the Christian is that one day the Church will see Jesus Christ.

About thirty years ago, God showed me a glimpse of the coming of our Lord Jesus Christ. In the dream I heard a very loud sound like a clash of cymbals that caught the attention of every human being I was able to see at that moment. Everyone stopped everything they were doing and looked toward where the sound had come from; behold, all eyes—including mine—followed the direction of the sound and looked toward heaven. What I saw amazed me; I saw the glory of God and the angels of God announcing the arrival of Jesus Christ, the King of all kings. I saw the Church jubilating and saying at last, "We are free; please come, Lord, we want to see you, Jesus."

Then I saw a group of people wailing and looking for a place to hide. They were crying and saying, "So it was true when Christ followers said that Christ was coming back again." They were devastated and full of bitter regret, for they hadn't accepted Jesus Christ as their Lord and personal Savior. Assuming they were able to turn the hand of the clock back, they would have done so. Thank God that Christ hasn't yet come; He is still waiting for that individual to repent, because He is ready to forgive you. Christians should be spiritually alert, watchful, and vigilant—and living as people who are wise.

When Christians look at what is going on around the Church and the world, there is that temptation to ask a lot of questions. One of the questions is, "Why is it that some people get away with evil that they commit even in the Church?" God ministered a word of encouragement that the Church shouldn't be tired of doing what is right. The truth is that Jesus Christ is coming back to judge both the Christian and nonChristian and that He is seeing what is happening all over the universe. He is coming to judge the world because He is seeing all the things men do. The Church should also realize that His grace is on both the godly and the ungodly.

God loves justice. He didn't want to see His people, the ones He'd created, be oppressed unjustly. That is why He delivers both Christians and nonChristian when they are oppressed. God is merciful, and He is full of compassion. He gives nonChristians time to repent; that is His desire for everyone. The Bible made the Church to understand that "the Lord is watching everywhere, keeping His eye on both the evil and the good" (Proverbs 15:3 NLT). Revelation 22:7–20 says,

> "Look, I am coming soon! Blessed is the one who keeps the words of the prophecy written in this scroll." I, John, am the one who heard and saw these things. And when I had heard and seen them, I fell down to worship at the feet of the angel who had been showing them to me. But he said to me, "Don't do that! I am a fellow servant with you and with your fellow prophets and with all who keep the words of this scroll. Worship God!" Then he told me, "Do not seal up the words of the prophecy of this scroll, because the time is near. Let the one who does wrong continue to do wrong; let the vile person continue to be vile; let the one who does right continue to do right; and let the holy person continue to be holy. Look, I am coming soon! My reward is with me, and I will give to each person according to what they have done. I am the Alpha and the Omega, the First and the Last, the Beginning and the End. Blessed are those who wash their robes, that they may have the right to the tree of life and may go through the gates into the city. Outside are the dogs, those who practice magic arts, the sexually immoral, the murderers, the idolaters and everyone who loves and practices falsehood. I, Jesus, have sent my angel to give you this testimony for the churches. I am the Root and the Offspring of David, and the bright Morning Star." The Spirit and the bride say, "Come!" And let the one who hears say, "Come!" Let the one who is thirsty come; and let the one who wishes take the free gift of the water of life. I warn everyone who hears the words of the prophecy of this scroll: If anyone adds anything to them, God will add to that person the

> plagues described in this scroll. And if anyone takes words away from this scroll of prophecy, God will take away from that person any share in the tree of life and in the Holy City, which are described in this scroll. He who testifies to these things says, "Yes, I am coming soon." Amen. Come, Lord Jesus (NIV).

The hope of seeing Jesus Christ and being in His presence must be the top priority in the heart of a believer. When Jesus Christ comes today, is the Church ready to meet Him? Believers will be rewarded by the Lord Jesus Christ according to our works. It is encouraging that Christians will be rewarded by God according to their works, which is a great achievement. That is why the Church should strive to walk in obedience with God by His grace.

Healings and miracles performed under the authority of the name of Jesus Christ can only stand the test of time. Repentance and holiness are what Christ demands from the Church. Acts 8:5–24 says,

> Philip went down to a city in Samaria and proclaimed the Messiah there. When the crowds heard Philip and saw the signs he performed, they all paid close attention to what he said. For with shrieks, impure spirits came out of many, and many who were paralyzed or lame were healed. So there was great joy in that city. Now for some time a man named Simon had practiced sorcery in the city and amazed all the people of Samaria. He boasted that he was someone great, and all the people, both high and low, gave him their attention and exclaimed, "This man is rightly called the Great Power of God." They followed him because he had amazed them for a long time with his sorcery. But when they believed Philip as he proclaimed the good news of the kingdom of God and the name of Jesus Christ, they were baptized, both men and women. *Simon himself believed and was baptized.* And he followed Philip everywhere, astonished by the great signs and miracles he

> saw. When the apostles in Jerusalem heard that Samaria had accepted the word of God, they sent Peter and John to Samaria. When they arrived, they prayed for the new believers there that they might receive the Holy Spirit, because the Holy Spirit had not yet come on any of them; they had simply been baptized in the name of the Lord Jesus. Then Peter and John placed their hands on them, and they received the Holy Spirit. When Simon saw that the Spirit was given at the laying on of the apostles' hands, he offered them money and said, "Give me also this ability so that everyone on whom I lay my hands may receive the Holy Spirit." Peter answered: "May your money perish with you, because you thought you could buy the gift of God with money! You have no part or share in this ministry, because your heart is not right before God. Repent of this wickedness and pray to the Lord in the hope that He may forgive you for having such a thought in your heart. For I see that you are full of bitterness and captive to sin." Then Simon answered, "Pray to the Lord for me so that nothing you have said may happen to me" (NIV, emphasis added).

In this passage we were told very clearly that Christ used the apostles to proclaim the good news about the kingdom of God, followed by signs and miracles. It is clearly stated in this passage to the Church that Christ's power cannot be bought with money or for anybody to practice sorcery to deceive people that the power is from Jesus Christ. Such an act is evil and very deceptive. Peter was able to rebuke Simon because he was filled with the power of the Holy Spirit. Peter did not rebuke him for his personal gain but because he knew who he was in Christ to always stand for the truth, which is in the Word of God. To live a successful Christian life, Christians must be truthful to themselves and to others to do what is right to be able to stand against what is evil.

The question is, are you using the right power that comes only from the Almighty God to preach, pray, and perform miracles? The Bible says, "But God's truth stands firm like a foundation stone with this inscription: 'The Lord knows those who are His and All who belong to the Lord must turn away from evil'" (2 Timothy 2:19 NLT). In Jesus Christ and through the power of the Holy Spirit alone, the Church will triumphantly walk in successful Christian lives.

1.2.4 Confidence

Hebrews 11:1 says, "Faith is the confidence that what we hope for will actually happen; it gives us assurance about things we cannot see" (NLT). Christ is the living hope; when the Church prays through Him, circumstances change. Jesus Christ is the confidence of the Church, on which the Christian stands. Hearing the Word of God over and over again builds the confidence of a Christian to live a Successful Christian life.

God will answer effective prayers. Having absolute faith in God is one aspect of the Bible that has really become real in my personal life by the grace of God. I have had several challenges in my life, and God has come through for me in each of them, demonstrating His power to provide, save, heal, and bless. Psalm 34:15–22 says,

> The eyes of the Lord are on the righteous, and His ears are attentive to their cry; but the face of the Lord is against those who do evil, to blot out their name from the earth. The righteous cry out, and the Lord hears them; He delivers them from all their troubles. The Lord is close to the brokenhearted and saves those who are crushed in spirit. The righteous person may have many troubles, but the Lord delivers him from them all; He protects all his bones, not one of them will be broken. Evil will slay the wicked; the foes of the righteous will be condemned. The Lord will rescue His servants; no one who takes refuge in Him will be condemned (NIV).

I encourage Christians to trust God concerning every aspect of their lives. The genuineness of your faith as Christ followers is based on your personal relationship with God. The followers of Christ know that confidence in God is very important to run the race, because pleasing God without confidence (faith) is impossible. The Word of God is the only source of a Christian's faith that can transform and change lives. Our faith will always be subject to testing and purification. The redeemed Christian knows that faith comes daily by hearing, studying the Word of God, and acting on it. James 2:14–26 says,

> What good is it, my brothers and sisters, if someone claims to have faith but has no deeds? Can such faith save them? Suppose a brother or a sister is without clothes and daily food. If one of you says to them, "Go in peace; keep warm and well fed," but does nothing about their physical needs, what good is it? In the same way, faith by itself, if it is not accompanied by action, is dead. But someone will say, "You have faith; I have deeds." Show me your faith without deeds, and I will show you my faith by my deeds. You believe that there is one God. Good! Even the demons believe that—and shudder. You foolish person, do you want evidence that faith without deeds is useless? Was not our father Abraham considered righteous for what he did when he offered his son Isaac on the altar? You see that his faith and his actions were working together, and his faith was made complete by what he did. And the scripture was fulfilled that says, "Abraham believed God, and it was credited to him as righteousness," and he was called God's friend. You see that a person is considered righteous by what they do and not by faith alone. In the same way, was not even Rahab the prostitute considered righteous for what she did when she gave lodging to the spies and sent them off in a different direction? As the body without the spirit is dead, so faith without deeds is dead (NIV).

According to God's Word, believing right without doing what is right cannot lead to success. Believing and doing what is right lead to living a successful Christian life. Faith in God and prayer go together. Jesus Christ demonstrated to the Church what we are supposed to do by studying the Word, praying, and acting on it. The committed Christian prays in the way that truly reveals his or her personal relationship with God the Father, because his or her total dependence is in Him alone.

The Church knows that with God all things are possible; that is why all needs should be taken to God in prayer, because He knows all things. Needs are met through prayer with the step of faith. God shows Himself powerful in His own ways. He will answer an earnest prayer to forgive sins, break chains, heal, and set the captives free and restore people when we; ask according to His will. Jesus Christ is the master of them all; He has given everything the Christian needs to live a godly and productive life. Confidence of living a successful Christian life is built on the success story of victory of our Lord Jesus Christ over the devil.

John 14:11–14 says, "Believe me when I say that I am in the Father and the Father is in me; or at least believe on the evidence of the works themselves. Very truly I tell you, whoever believes in me will do the works I have been doing, and they will do even greater things than these, because I am going to the Father. And I will do whatever you ask in my name, so that the Father may be glorified in the Son. You may ask me for anything in my name, and I will do it" (NIV). The Bible also says, "For God hath not given us the Spirit of fear; but of power and of love, and of a sound mind." (Second Timothy 1:7 KJV) What is in your mind, and what controls you?

These are assuring words from the Lord Jesus Christ; the words of God are sure and amen. The assuring words of Jesus Christ to the Church are that any Christian who believes in the works He has done will do a greater work in His name. Jesus Christ has given the Church the authority of His name to be used to ask anything according to His will. He assured us with His Word that He will do it. The Church can only achieve this by the power of the Holy Spirit that drives away fear. It is a success when prayers are answered by God.

1.2.5 Exalted

Psalm 18:46 says, "The Lord lives! Praise to my Rock! May the God of my salvation be exalted!" (NLT).

"O magnify the Lord with me, and let us exalt His name together" (Psalm 34:3 KJV). How pleasant it is to see the body of Christ coming together to elevate and glorify the Almighty God. He is the ruler and controller of all things.

One of the secrets of living a successful Christian life is showing appreciation to God by telling others how big God is and what He is capable of doing in every situation. I encourage the Church—don't quit praising and exalting the Lord; even if you are in your dark moment now, you are not alone. The storm will be calm by His grace. Praise your way through, because God will surely come to deliver you. Hallelujah! Songs and praises bring honor to Him, and He feels delighted with the Church when believers do that.

According to the Bible, King David was a man after God's heart. He knew how to exalt God with dance, worship, praises, and even prayer. He always called on the name of the Lord in every step he took. As a king he was willing to do whatever God had told him to do to please Him. King David made mistakes and even sinned, but that's what made him different: he recognized that he had sinned but decided not to justify his actions. He humbled himself before the Lord and prayed to God to have mercy on him. The Lord forgave him, because David admitted his sins, pleaded for mercy, and repented. David was always praising and exalting the name of God before presenting his needs to the almighty God.

He was successful as a king because of his obedience and willingness to work with God. He knew how to adore and praise God. The name of the Lord must be exalted in the midst of the people of God. We Christians need total surrender to see the power of God move and much more when we, as a body of Christ, come together in worship to exalt Him. Appreciation to God gives the Christian a bigger view of who God is. To honor God will be the lifestyle and the natural thing to do as a Christian because the Lord lives and is very much alive in the hearts of those who sincerely seek Him.

Let the name of God be exalted in our prayers, songs, worship, praises, and dances to honor Him. "Jesus Christ is exalted to the place of highest honor in heaven, at God's right hand. The reason why God must be exalted above any other name is that He declared Himself to Moses in Exodus 3:14a (KJV). "And God said unto Moses, 'I Am That I Am…'" That is His name. He is the almighty God, the merciful God, the Healer, the Rock of Ages, the Living Word, the Bread of Life. He has no equal. He is the Fountain of Life, the First and the Last, the Beginning and the End, the Chancellor, the Living Water, the Lion of the tribe of Judah, and the Faithful One. Christians are obligated to be true worshipers of God Almighty, if they realize deep in their hearts who God is. To live a successful Christian life, we, the Church as a body of Christ, must humble ourselves before the almighty God and exalt Him in everything we do.

1.2.6 Salvation

There is no salvation in anyone else than Jesus Christ. Salvation of God through Jesus Christ is the genuine price Jesus fully paid on the cross on our behalf for our sins. Through the blood of Jesus Christ and the testimony of His Word, the Church is redeemed. Salvation is the key word, which means the finished work of God to rescue man from the stronghold of sin and eternal condemnation. The Lord provides light and safety in the time of distress. His hand is mighty to save and to deliver. Romans 1:18–30 says,

> The wrath of God is being revealed from heaven against all the godlessness and wickedness of people, who suppress the truth by their wickedness, since what may be known about God is plain to them, because God has made it plain to them. For since the creation of the world God's invisible qualities—His eternal power and divine nature—have been clearly seen, being understood from what has been made, so that people are without excuse.

> For although they knew God, they neither glorified Him as God nor gave thanks to Him, but their thinking became futile and their foolish hearts were darkened. Although they claimed to be wise, they became fools and exchanged the glory of the immortal God for images made to look like a mortal human being and birds and animals and reptiles. Therefore God gave them over in the sinful desires of their hearts to sexual impurity for the degrading of their bodies with one another. They exchanged the truth about God for a lie, and worshiped and served created things rather than the Creator—who is forever praised. Amen. Because of this, God gave them over to shameful lusts. Even their women exchanged natural sexual relations for unnatural ones. In the same way the men also abandoned natural relations with women and were inflamed with lust for one another. Men committed shameful acts with other men, and received in themselves the due penalty for their sin. Furthermore, just as they did not think it worthwhile to retain the knowledge of God, so God gave them over to a depraved mind, so that they do what ought not to be done. They have become filled with every kind of wickedness, evil, greed and depravity. They are full of envy, murder, strife, deceit and malice. They are gossips, slanderers, God-haters, insolent, arrogant and boastful; they invent ways of doing evil; they disobey their parents (NIV).

The book of Romans made it clear that sin angers God. The Holy Bible reveals the wrath of God against anyone that is ungodly and filled with any kind of wickedness. The only respite from His wrath is repenting from any kind of sin and accepting Jesus Christ as Lord and personal savior. Man has no excuse to indulge in sinful acts because God gave everyone the opportunity to receive the free gift of salvation that He offered to man through Jesus Christ. God is willing to forgive any individual, no matter how heavy the sin is, as long as the person is willing to repent. Sin is not only a barrier in your walk with God, but it also separates

the individual from God. That is why we as bodies of the Church must run away from sin by confessing it to the Lord so that He will take over our minds. Who is in control of your mind? Give your mind and your heart to Jesus in order to live a successful Christian life.
Titus 2:11–15 says,

> For the grace of God has been revealed, bringing salvation to all people. And we are instructed to turn from godless living and sinful pleasures. We should live in this evil world with wisdom, righteousness, and devotion to God, while we look forward with hope to that wonderful day when the glory of our great God and Savior, Jesus Christ, will be revealed. He gave His life to free us from every kind of sin, to cleanse us, and to make us His very own people, totally committed to doing good deeds. You must teach these things and encourage the believers to do them (NLT).

Psalm 62:2 says, "He alone is my rock and my salvation, my fortress where I will never be shaken" (NLT).

To have fellowship with Christians, without individuals receiving the free salvation Christ offers, is impossible. One cannot live a successful Christian life in this way. God is calling that individual to receive the gift of salvation by total repentance and surrender to Him.

1.2.7 Shepherd

Psalm 23:1 says, "The Lord is my shepherd; I have all that I need" (NLT).

True loyalty comes with obedience in following the Good Shepherd to live a successful Christian life. The body of Christ is encouraged to be loyal to God Almighty, because all the Church needs is found in Him alone. The devoted Christian will have the ultimate satisfaction by being loyal to His leadership. John 10:11–18 says,

> I am the good shepherd. The good shepherd lays down His life for the sheep. The hired hand is not the shepherd and does not own the sheep. So when he sees the wolf coming, he abandons the sheep and runs away. Then the wolf attacks the flock and scatters it. The man runs away because he is a hired hand and cares nothing for the sheep. I am the good shepherd; I know my sheep and my sheep know me—just as the Father knows me and I know the Father—and I lay down my life for the sheep. I have other sheep that are not of this sheep pen. I must bring them also. They too will listen to my voice, and there shall be one flock and one shepherd. The reason my Father loves me is that I lay down my life—only to take it up again. No one takes it from me, but I lay it down of my own accord. I have authority to lay it down and authority to take it up again. This command I received from my Father (NIV).

Jesus Christ is the only shepherd who is truthful and won't mislead His Church; He is the Good Shepherd and the faithful one. What devoted Christians have realized in living as successful Christians is that they have recognized Jesus Christ alone as their true shepherd and true source as their provider. They have also exhibited total surrender to His leading. In this regard devoted Christians recognize that Jesus Christ is in total control and in charge of every aspect of their lives.

1.2.8 Faithful

Deuteronomy 7:9 says, "Understand, therefore, that the Lord your God is indeed God. He is the *faithful* God who keeps His covenant for a thousand generations and lavishes His unfailing love on those who love Him and obey His commands" (NLT, emphasis added).

As a Church, Christians should individually and collectively be faithful to their commitment in serving God with their resources and time. The followers of Christ can testify of a truth that God is faithful. God is faithful to His name because He is the same God yesterday, today, and forever. By the grace of God, Christians are expected to be faithful to Him in their walk with God to be successful.

Luke 12:42–48 says,

> The Lord answered, "Who then is the faithful and wise manager, whom the master puts in charge of his servants to give them their food allowance at the proper time? It will be good for that servant whom the master finds doing so when he returns. Truly I tell you, he will put him in charge of all his possessions. But suppose the servant says to himself, 'My master is taking a long time in coming,' and he then begins to beat the other servants, both men and women, and to eat and drink and get drunk. The master of that servant will come on a day when he does not expect him and at an hour he is not aware of. He will cut him to pieces and assign him a place with the unbelievers. The servant who knows the master's will and does not get ready or does not do what the master wants will be beaten with many blows. But the one who does not know and does things deserving punishment will be beaten with few blows. From everyone who has been given much, much will be demanded; and from the one who has been entrusted with much, much more will be asked" (NIV).

The Church is reminded again that the Lord will come unexpectedly to take His children home to reign with Him. Will the Lord meet His Church still faithful? This is the time for spiritual awakening and revival in the Church. The Church needs to be alert and be watchful for children that are wise. Christians will be accountable to God for what He has entrusted into their hands. Christians are all servants of the Lord. Much will be expected by the Lord, especially from the leaders. When the Church remains faithful in using talents and gifts to honor God, there will be celebration with Christ when He comes. Don't be tired of waiting; hold on to His promise that Christ is coming back again.

What has God entrusted into your hands, my brothers and sisters? This is the time for reflection.

1.2.9 Upright

Deuteronomy 32:4 says, "He is the Rock; His deeds are perfect. Everything He does is just and fair. He is a faithful God who does no wrong; how *just and upright* He is!" (NLT, emphasis added).

God's ways are perfect and upright toward humanity because His thoughts for everyone are good. His plans are without mistakes and that is why His deeds are upright. Whatever God has done is for the good of humanity. His ways cannot be questioned because He is always right.

The Christian who desires to be successful in his or her walk with God knows that God has given the Church His words to live by, words of a moral standard and integrity. The only way the Christian can live in that expectation is by His grace and by total commitment because God-fearing people know their help comes from the Lord. He told us clearly in His Word to be holy as He is holy. As a body of Christ, we can live holy lives by the power of His Holy Spirit. It is true because He said so, and His Word cannot return to Him void. The Word of God describes the upright; the Lord delights in the prayers of the upright. He also blesses the home of the upright. The good thing is that when a Christian lives in such a way that brings honor to God, God releases His blessings in the home of the upright. David said, "I was young and now I am old, yet I have never seen the righteous forsaken or their children begging bread" (Psalm 37:25 NIV). The committed Christian knows that the source of his or her blessings is God alone. Deuteronomy 8:18 says, "Remember the Lord your God. He is the one who gives you power to be successful, in order to fulfill the covenant He confirmed to your ancestors with an oath" (NLT).

God confirmed His Word with an oath and tells the Church that He has our best interest in His heart. At times the Church forgets that God knows our needs much better than we do ourselves. The committed Christian desires to live an upright life to honor God because success comes with such a lifestyle.

1.2.10 Life

John 6:32–35 says, "Jesus said to them, 'Very truly I tell you, it is not Moses who has given you the bread from heaven, but it is my Father who gives you the true bread from heaven. For the bread of God is the bread that comes down from heaven and gives life to the world.' 'Sir,' they said, 'always gives us this bread.' Then Jesus declared, 'I am the bread of life. Whoever comes to me will never go hungry, and whoever believes in me will never be thirsty'" (NIV).

Jesus Christ declares Himself the Bread of Life and also the resurrection and the life. He has the power to give and to take life. Jesus Christ is life Himself. The Church's spiritual nourishment is the Bread of Life, the person of Jesus Christ, who is the Word of God. To live a successful Christian life, the Church must be devoted to the Word of God. Living a successful Christian life is possible only in Christ Jesus.

John 14:6–7 says, "Jesus answered, 'I am the way and the truth and the life. No one comes to the Father except through me. If you really know me, you will know my Father as well. From now on, you do know Him and have seen Him'" (NIV).

Without Him there is no meaningful life. Successful Christians have a solid confidence in God through Jesus Christ by studying the Word of God, which is life to the body, soul, and mind. Satisfaction and fulfillment come from the person of Jesus Christ. The Church rejoices in the living Word of God because there is life in Him.

1.2.11 Commandments

Devoted Christians know that the Word of God is from Genesis to Revelation. Thank God that the Head of the Church, Jesus Christ, came to fulfill the law. Matthew 5:17–20 says,

> Do not think that I have come to abolish the Law or the Prophets; I have not come to abolish them but to fulfill them. For truly I tell you, until heaven and earth disappear, not the smallest letter, not the least stroke of a pen,

> will by any means disappear from the Law until everything is accomplished. Therefore anyone who sets aside one of the least of these commands and teaches others accordingly will be called least in the kingdom of heaven, but whoever practices and teaches these commands will be called great in the kingdom of heaven. For I tell you that unless your righteousness surpasses that of the Pharisees and the teachers of the law, you will certainly not enter the kingdom of heaven (NIV).

Christians realize that everything God has given to the Church is free, but what He demands from us is that we obey Him. The Lord showed me something about the Church in a dream on May 18, 2013. I saw some group of people in the Church selling tickets for a church-organized crusade that would be coming up soon. God put these words in my mouth, because I know I cannot speak on my own without His leading. I told the group of people selling tickets that something wasn't right because it wasn't supposed to be so by selling tickets for the crusade. I told them that the purpose of the crusade had been defeated because the good news had been given to us freely—and freely we should give it. I asked them this question: "What are the tithes and offerings used for? The tithes and the offering should be used for the ministry to help the needy and to propagate the Word of God." Malachi 3:6–12 says,

> "I the Lord do not change. So you, the descendants of Jacob, are not destroyed. Ever since the time of your ancestors you have turned away from my decrees and have not kept them. Return to me, and I will return to you," says the Lord Almighty. "But you ask, 'How are we to return?' Will a mere mortal rob God? Yet you rob me. But you ask, 'How are we robbing you?' In tithes and offerings. You are under a curse—your whole nation—because you are robbing me. Bring the whole tithe into the storehouse, that there may be food in my house. Test me in this," says the Lord Almighty, "and see if I will not throw open the floodgates

of heaven and pour out so much blessing that there will not be room enough to store it. I will prevent pests from devouring your crops, and the vines in your fields will not drop their fruit before it is ripe," says the Lord Almighty. "Then all the nations will call you blessed, for yours will be a delightful land," says the Lord Almighty (NIV).

The primary aim of the Church is not to make profit but to win souls. The gathering of the body of Christ is not a place for personal business. If the idea to organize a crusade, prayer meetings, retreats, and several activities is to make money, then they are not of God.

John 14:15 says, "If you love me, obey my commandments" (NLT).

Profit making in church-organized events is not one of His commands. The business of God is about salvation, prayer, and the power of His Word preached around the globe and also from the pulpit to deliver people from every aspect of bondage.

Matthew 21:12–14 says, "Then Jesus went into the temple of God and drove out all those who bought and sold in the temple, and overturned the tables of the money changers and the seats of those who sold doves. And He said to them, 'It is written, "My house shall be called a house of prayer," but you have made it a "den of thieves."' Then the blind and the lame came to Him in the temple, and He healed them" (NKJV).

To be successful in walking with God, the individual allows God to build his or her character with His Word daily. The laws of God have been written in our hearts to do according to His will, through the power of the Holy Spirit. The Bible says, "Do not conform to the pattern of this world, but be transformed by the renewing of your mind. Then you will be able to test and approve what is—His good, pleasing and perfect will" Romans 12:2 (NIV).

1.2.12 Honor

First Corinthians 6:20 say, "For God bought you with a high price. So you must honor God with your body" (NLT).

The Holy Bible made us, the Church, to understand that our bodies belong not to us but only to God. Understanding the complete knowledge of the will of God through the power of the Holy Spirit will enable Christians to live in a way that honors God by pleasing Him and being productive. God-fearing people honor Him with their talents, wealth, service to God, and humanity. Christians also honor God with the way they dress.

Psalm 29:1–4 says, "Honor the Lord, you heavenly beings, honor the Lord for His glory and strength. Honor the Lord for the glory of His name. Worship the Lord in the splendor of His holiness. The voice of the Lord echoes above the sea. The God of glory thunders. The Lord thunders over the mighty sea. The voice of the Lord is powerful; the voice of the Lord is majestic" (NLT).

Romans 12:1 says, "And so dear brothers and sisters, I plead with you to give your bodies to God because of all He has done for you. Let them be a living and holy sacrifice—the kind He will find acceptable. This is truly the way to worship Him" (NLT).

1.2.13 Remain

Jesus said in John 15:1–17,

> I am the true vine, and my Father is the gardener. He cuts off every branch in me that bears no fruit, while every branch that does bear fruit He prunes so that it will be even more fruitful. You are already clean because of the word I have spoken to you. *Remain in me,* as I also *remain in you.* No branch can bear fruit by itself; it must remain in the vine. Neither can you bear fruit unless you remain in me. I am the vine; you are the branches. If you remain in me and I in you, you will bear much fruit; apart from me you can do nothing. If you do not remain in me, you are like a branch that is thrown away and withers; such branches are picked up, thrown into the fire and burned. If you remain in me and my words remain in you, ask whatever you wish, and it will be done for you. This is to my Father's glory, that you bear much fruit, showing

> yourselves to be my disciples. As the Father has loved me, so have I loved you. Now remain in my love. If you keep my commands, you will remain in my love, just as I have kept my Father's commands and remain in His love. I have told you this so that my joy may be in you and that your joy may be complete. My command is this: Love each other as I have loved you. Greater love has no one than this: to lay down one's life for one's friends. You are my friends if you do what I command. I no longer call you servants, because a servant does not know his master's business. Instead, I have called you friends, for everything that I learned from my Father I have made known to you. You did not choose me, but I chose you and appointed you so that you might go and bear fruit—fruit that will last—and so that whatever you ask in my name the Father will give you. This is my command: Love each other (NIV, emphasis added).

To live a successful Christian life, the Church needs to understand that God chose us, not just to be His followers alone but also to bear fruit worthy of repentance to impact lives continuously. The Church cannot be productive without obeying God. To succeed as a Christian, individuals in the Church must learn how to remain in Christ and to confide in Him. It is only the Word of God that can nourish a Christian to be fruitful. When the Church continues to stay in the presence of God, it will result in prayers being answered. No matter how long it takes, God will honor His Word. The joy that is sustainable and lasting to eternity comes only from the person of Jesus Christ when the Church remains in Him. To remain in Christ, Christians are encouraged to study the Word of God personally, to grow, and to be nurtured daily to live a successful life. The Word of God is not just ordinary words. The Holy Bible is not like any other book, because God's Word is powerful and alive.

Hebrews 4:12 says, "For the Word of God is alive and powerful, it is sharper than the sharpest two-edged sword, cutting between soul and spirit, between joint and marrow. It exposes our innermost thoughts and desires" (NLT).

The Church is encouraged to read the Word with divine understanding because that is the only way it can be effective in the life of a believer. Speak the Word of God daily into your life because His Word is life changing. God has given the Church His Word as our weapon against the strategies of the devil. Having faith in the Word of God and praying without ceasing, the Church is able to quench all the fiery darts of the enemy against the people of God. If you confide in the Lord and take your burdens to Him, you will experience peace that comes from the love of God. Real love is the love of Christ that is pure and holy. The Church is encouraged to love one another because it is a command from God. The love of God is not a feeling but is an expression of who God is.

In Matthew 11:28 Jesus said, "Come to me, all of you who are weary and carry heavy burdens, and I will give you rest" (NLT). To function daily the success of a Christian depends on the power and strength of God.

1.2.14 Inscription

Second Timothy 2:19 says, "But God's truth stands firm like a foundation stone with this inscription: 'The Lord knows those who are His,' and 'All who belong to the Lord must turn away from evil'" (NLT). The Word of God has been inscribed in the hearts of those who fear God so they can live successful Christian lives. Christians detest evil, through the power of the Holy Spirit, because they recognize who they are in Christ Jesus. The name of the Lord is inscribed in the hearts of Christians as a mark of total surrender to His will. These Christians carry God's tabernacles and His presence because they are God-fearing people who run away from evil. Proverbs 6:16–23 says,

> There are six things the Lord hates, seven that are detestable to Him: haughty eyes, a lying tongue, hands that shed innocent blood, a heart that devises wicked schemes, feet

> that are quick to rush into evil, a false witness who pours out lies and a person who stirs up conflict in the community. My son, keep your father's command and do not forsake your mother's teaching. Bind them always on your heart; fasten them around your neck. When you walk, they will guide you; when you sleep, they will watch over you; when you awake, they will speak to you. For this command is a lamp, this teaching is a light, and correction and instruction are the way to life (NIV).

Evil is in opposition to the will of God; that is why the Church must detest evil and not encourage it in any form.

1.2.15 Seed

God's desire for the Church is to impact lives. Luke 8:4–17 says,

> While a large crowd was gathering and people were coming to Jesus from town after town, He told this parable: "A farmer went out to sow his seed. As he was scattering the seed, some fell along the path; it was trampled on, and the birds ate it up. Some fell on rocky ground, and when it came up, the plants withered because they had no moisture. Other seed fell among thorns, which grew up with it and choked the plants. Still other seed fell on good soil. It came up and yielded a crop, a hundred times more than was sown." When He said this, He called out, "Whoever has ears to hear, let them hear." His disciples asked Him what this parable meant. He said, "The knowledge of the secrets of the kingdom of God has been given to you, but to others I speak in parables, so that, 'though seeing, they may not see; though hearing, they may not understand.' This is the meaning of the parable: The seed is the word of God. Those along the path are the ones who hear, and then the devil comes and takes away the word from their hearts, so that they may not believe and be saved. Those on the rocky ground are the ones who receive the word with

> joy when they hear it, but they have no root. They believe for a while, but in the time of testing they fall away. The seed that fell among thorns stands for those who hear, but as they go on their way they are choked by life's worries, riches and pleasures, and they do not mature. But the seed on good soil stands for those with a noble and good heart, who hear the word, retain it, and by persevering produce a crop. No one lights a lamp and hides it in a clay jar or puts it under a bed. Instead, they put it on a stand, so that those who come in can see the light. For there is nothing hidden that will not be disclosed, and nothing concealed that will not be known or brought out into the open" (NIV).

In this passage Jesus tells us of a parable on the various ways in which the Word of God is received. For one reason or the other, some drifted away because they could not retain His Word in their hearts. Some drifted because of unbelief, and some were not rooted in the Word of God. Some drifted because of worries, riches, and pleasures that prevented them from maturing in the Word of God. The seed, which is the Word of God, has an important role in the life of a Christian. How an individual receives the Word of God is very important in living a successful Christian life. Personal conviction in your heart on how you hear and receive the Word of God is the key role to Christianity. Jesus Christ tells this parable for us, the Church, to reflect on and be truthful to and ask ourselves; is the Church still operating in the power of His Word today? The seed that was sown in your heart, when you heard the Word of God and received Christ with joy—what happened to it? Suddenly you have now become very busy or have other priorities that do not involve studying the Word of God. What that leads to is a certain emptiness within an individual. The empty heart will be taken over by the devil because the power of God cannot operate in an empty heart. To guard against it, let the Word of God be your companion. Are you in the category of the individual that just fellowships with other believers because you have to? Or do you see the followership as a social gathering? You are encouraged to go back to God and ask for His forgiveness and repent. God will forgive you so that His Word can be brought to life in your heart in order to live a successful Christian life. It is the Word of God that cleans and purifies the heart of a Christian and leads the believer to do good works. The truth is that when the Church perseveres and is rooted in God's Word, His Word will shine through His Church, thus producing noble characters and pure hearts within.

1.2.16 Thanksgiving

Jesus prayed a prayer of thanksgiving to teach us the importance of how to be thankful to God. Luke 10:21–24 says,

> At that time Jesus, full of joy through the Holy Spirit, said, "I praise you, Father, Lord of heaven and earth, because you have hidden these things from the wise and learned, and revealed them to little children. Yes, Father, for this is what you were pleased to do. All things have been committed to me by my Father. No one knows who the Son is except the Father, and no one knows who the Father is except the Son and those to whom the Son chooses to reveal Him." Then He turned to His disciples and said privately, "Blessed are the eyes that see what you see. For I tell you that many prophets and kings wanted to see what you see but did not see it, and to hear what you hear but did not hear it" (NIV).

The Christian should remember to express thanks to God with a heart of gratitude, acknowledging Him and celebrating God's goodness. The Christian should realize that life is a gift, not a right, especially the gift of salvation; and then the mind-set of the Church will change to begin every gathering with songs and prayers of thanksgiving to the Lord. The Church should acknowledge God first, with the heart of thanksgiving, in everything. Psalm 100:4 says, "Enter His gates with thanksgiving; go into His courts with praise. Give thanks to Him and praise His name" (NLT).

King David acknowledged God in all circumstances, trials, battles, and victories. King David was a man after God's own heart, and, for that, his walk with God was successful. First Samuel 18:14 says, "David continued to succeed in everything he did, for the Lord was with him" (NLT). He remembered when God had come through for him. He said in Psalm 103:1–3, "Praise the Lord, my soul; all my inmost being, praise His holy name. Praise the Lord, my soul, and forget not all His benefits—who forgives all your sins and heals all your diseases" (NIV).

Whether prayers are answered, we, the body of Christ, should thank Him for what He is already doing. Living a successful Christian life demands every believer to praise Him and to be thankful. Luke 17:11–19 says,

> Now on His way to Jerusalem, Jesus traveled along the border between Samaria and Galilee. As He was going into a village, ten men who had leprosy met Him. They stood at a distance and called out in a loud voice, "Jesus, Master, have pity on us!" When He saw them, He said, "Go, and show yourselves to the priests." And as they went, they were cleansed. One of them, when he saw he was healed, came back, praising God in a loud voice. He threw himself at Jesus' feet and thanked Him—and he was a Samaritan. Jesus asked, "Were not all ten cleansed? Where are the other nine? Has no one returned to give praise to God except this foreigner?" Then He said to him, "Rise and go; your faith has made you well" (NIV).

Christians can praise their way to success. The Church is encouraged to testify what God has done in their lives and remember to thank Him. One of the lepers came back to tell Jesus thank you, when he saw that he was heal by Jesus Christ. That was amazing and is commendable because Jesus Christ was pleased with that single act. Let the Church always be thankful to God Almighty because it is a noble thing to do.

1.2.17 Insight

Ephesians 1:17 says, "I keep asking that the God of our Lord Jesus Christ, the glorious Father, may give you the Spirit of wisdom and revelation, so that you may know Him better" (NIV). A great insight of the Word of God is necessary for spiritual growth to be successful in the Christian race. The wisdom of the Word of God makes the spirit of discernment in the life of a Christian very active and vigilant in any situation. To be successful in spiritual matters, it is the Word of God that gives insight. Psalm 19:8 says, "The precepts of the Lord are right, giving joy to the heart. The commands of the Lord are radiant, giving light to the eyes" (NIV).

A Christian's vision is sharpening to new insight daily as he or she walks with God. The followers of Christ have unshakable insight about the Word of God, which is alive, powerful, active, and vibrant in their hearts. Proverbs 7:4 says, "Say to wisdom, 'You are my sister,' and to insight, 'You are my relative'" (NIV). Without insight into the Word of God, things can go wrong and be misleading. Insight is one of the ways to become successful as a Christian.

1.2.18 Authority

Authority to do the will and the work of God comes from Him alone. The Church can operate only under the authority of our Lord and Savior Jesus Christ to be recognized by God the Father. God has given the Church the ability and authority of His Word to pray, preach, and do good deeds. Every other authority is subject to the authority of God. As a result we have been given authority by God over Satan and his agents. Luke 10:17–20 says, "The seventy-two returned with joy and said, 'Lord, even the demons submit to us in your name.' He replied, 'I saw Satan fall like lightning from heaven. I have given you authority to trample on snakes and scorpions and to overcome all the power of the enemy; nothing will harm you. However, do not rejoice that the spirits submit to you, but rejoice that your names are written in heaven'" (NIV).

Any Church that doesn't stand under the authority of the name of Jesus Christ to pray, teach, preach, evangelize, and perform miracles is on its own. God has given the Church the weapon of His Word as the authority of the Christian. Second Corinthians 10:4–5 says, "The weapons we fight with are not the weapons of the world. On the contrary, they have divine power to demolish strongholds. We demolish arguments and every pretension that sets itself up against the knowledge of God, and we take captive every thought to make it obedient to Christ" (NIV).

1.2.19 News

Romans 1:16 says, "For I am not ashamed of this Good News about Christ. It is the power of God at work, saving everyone who believes—the Jew first and also the Gentile" (NLT).

This verse means Jesus Christ is the good news; without Him the Church can do nothing. Christ followers cannot be ashamed of this good news because it is the source of the Church's power of God at work within us. The Word of God is a special revelation from Almighty God. News can be overlooked when an individual is unconcerned, but this good news, according to the Holy Bible, is about repenting and accepting what Jesus Christ has done for humanity, because it stands the test of time. This news cannot be ignored, because it commands everyone's attention.

Christians must not drift from the message of the good news, because it is all about the kingdom of God. The good news is about Jesus Christ and how He came to show the world the road to live a successful life. John 3:16–21 says this is good news.

> For God loved the world so much that He gave His one and only Son, so that everyone who believes in Him will not perish but have eternal life. God sent His Son into the world not to judge the world, but to save the world through Him. There is no judgment against anyone who believes in Him. But anyone who does not believe in Him has already been judged for not believing in God's one and only Son. And the judgment is based on this fact:

> God's light came into the world, but people loved the darkness more than the light, for their actions were evil. All who do evil hate the light and refuse to go near it for fear their sins will be exposed. But those who do what is right come to the light so others can see that they are doing what God wants (NLT).

The Christian knows that the power and love of God demonstrated to mankind are found in the good news. Mark 16:15–18 says, "He said to them, 'Go into all the world and preach the gospel to all creation. Whoever believes and is baptized will be saved, but whoever does not believe will be condemned. And these signs will accompany those who believe: In my name they will drive out demons; they will speak in new tongues; they will pick up snakes with their hands; and when they drink deadly poison, it will not hurt them at all; they will place their hands on sick people, and they will get well'" (NIV).

That is why Christians must give Him the due respect in everything because Jesus Christ gave all to them to operate in His power. He renewed the minds and the hearts of anyone who embraced His love. The good news is that He paid all the debts of humanity. He is the burden bearer and the living water. His words are not misleading but lead to a good and successful life. He is not limited in His resources to forgive.

God is faithful and upright in what He does. God came to give us life through the death of His Son, Jesus Christ, who rose from the dead to deliver the Church from every stronghold of Satan. Accepting the Lord Jesus Christ means repenting from sins and turning away from evil. Successful Christians realize they are representatives of the kingdom of God as true ambassadors of Jesus Christ.

Living a successful Christian life means abiding under the principles and values of God Almighty. Anytime and anywhere, believers should be identified as God-fearing individuals, doing exactly what they believe is what Jesus Christ instructs. The followers of Christ are not double minded; they do not compromise the Word of God. Their focus is to preach the good news—which is centered on Jesus Christ alone.

1.3ExamplesofPeople WhoSuccessfullyWorkedwithGod

In the Bible there are many examples of people who walked with God and were very successful. Here are a few examples we will discuss: Abraham, Moses, Joshua, Samuel, Daniel, and the apostle Paul. These people made mistakes, but what made them different was their sincerity in their walk with God. They were honest in their individual callings.

Abraham

According to the Bible, God called Abraham, the father of many nations, from a pagan home to a land he didn't know. God appeared to Abraham and said He was El Shaddai, God Almighty. God gave Abraham His word that if he served Him faithfully and lived a blameless life, God would bless him. Here are a few distinguishing features in Abraham's walk with God:

- His prior pagan gods kept him only in penury, poverty, and hopelessness before he encountered God.
- He became wealthy materially during his walk with God.
- Old age didn't define his ability to give birth to children, contrary to human wisdom.
- He successfully fought wars; he rescued Lot when he was taken captive.

He obeyed God, left the idols behind, and took God for His word. Abraham had faith in God, and because of his obedience, he was very successful. He had faith in God, and God counted it to him for righteousness. There is power in obedience. God is moved to action when a Christian truly obeys His word. Abraham left his footprint by building altars wherever the Lord appeared to him. He recognized God and also had a thankful heart.

Moses

God sent Moses to Egypt to meet Pharaoh. God gave Moses His word and demonstrated His awesome power in Egypt through Moses. Moses lacked confidence before his encounter with God. God introduced Himself to Moses "God replied to Moses, "I AM WHO I AM.* Say this to the people of Israel: I Am has sent me to you." "God also said to Moses, "Say this to the people of Israel: Yahweh,* the God of your ancestors—the God of Abraham, the God of Isaac, and the God of Jacob – has sent me to you." (Exodus 3:14-15 NLT)

There was a dramatic turnaround in his confidence and boldness after his encounter with God. He engaged Pharaoh on behalf of the people of Israel without fear. He went to Egypt confidently because he had heard from God. He knew that the perfect pursuit is the true pursuit for God. Moses went on that mission, not to speak his own word. God gave His word to Moses, and he went to Egypt to deliver the message to the people of Israel and to introduce the name of God to them. Exodus 4:14 says, "God replied to Moses 'I AM WHO I AM' say this to the people of Israel: I AM has sent me to you" (NLT). God empowered Moses and He backed His word and that mission was successful. Moses was successful because he walked according to God's instructions. The importance of knowing the God we serve and working according to His dictates cannot be overemphasized.

Joshua

Joshua took over from Moses to lead the Israelites to Canaan, the Promised Land. To successfully work with God, you need to be filled with the spirit of wisdom and serve faithfully. Deuteronomy 34:9 says, "Now Joshua son of Nun was filled with the spirit of wisdom because Moses had laid his hands on him" (NLT).

So the Israelites listened to him and did what the Lord had commanded Moses. God used Joshua to successfully fight many battles. God gave him victory because Joshua obeyed Him. He led the Israelites across the Jordan, attacked and conquered the Canaanites, and divided up the land among his followers.

Before every battle Joshua sought the face of God for approval. Joshua understood perfectly the importance of walking with God wholeheartedly, especially in the area of seeking His face before embarking on any endeavor. Joshua and his family chose to serve the Lord. He declared, "I and my house shall serve the Lord," which means he knew his God personally.

Do you know God personally? Have you deliberately chosen to serve Him? Joshua is calling us to action today: Joshua 24:14–15 says, "Now fear the Lord and serve Him with all faithfulness. Throw away the gods your ancestors worshiped beyond the Euphrates River and in Egypt, and serve the Lord. But if serving the Lord seems undesirable to you, then choose for yourselves this day whom you will serve, whether the gods your ancestors served beyond the Euphrates, or the gods of the Amorites, in whose land you are living. But as for me and my household, we will serve the Lord" (NIV). Joshua held his people to high standards of personal conduct, admonishing them to serve and honor God. Joshua 10:10–12 says,

> The Lord threw them into confusion before Israel, so Joshua and the Israelites defeated them completely at Gibeon. Israel pursued them along the road going up to Beth Horon and cut them down all the way to Azekah and Makkedah. As they fled before Israel on the road down from Beth Horon to Azekah, the Lord hurled large hailstones down on them, and more of them died from the hail than were killed by the swords of the Israelites. On the day the Lord gave the Amorites over to Israel, Joshua said to the Lord in the presence of Israel: "Sun, stand still over Gibeon, and you, moon, over the Valley of Aijalon" (NIV).

God never loses any battle, especially when a Christian is loyal and follows His instructions. God takes every battle personally when the Church submits to Him for His name to be glorified. Joshua succeeded in his walk with God because he was loyal to

God and backed his actions with prayers for a total trust in God. For any individual to live a successful Christian life, that person must be devoted to God alone.

Apostle Paul

The life of the apostle Paul tells a message to the Church. No matter what calling God has given to a Christian, the evidence is obvious, because it's not the individual who does the work but the power of Christ in him or her.

Paul's focus was not on miracles but on the person of Jesus Christ and the miracles that followed. The chief priest tried to do what Paul was doing by his own strength, and the evil spirit told him, "Jesus I know, and Paul I know about, but who are you?" What makes the difference is Jesus Christ, when the Church operates in His presence. Acts 19:11–20 says,

> God did extraordinary miracles through Paul, so that even handkerchiefs and aprons that had touched him were taken to the sick, and their illnesses were cured and the evil spirits left them. Some Jews who went around driving out evil spirits tried to invoke the name of the Lord Jesus over those who were demon-possessed. They would say, "In the name of the Jesus whom Paul preaches, I command you to come out." Seven sons of Sceva, a Jewish chief priest, were doing this. One day the evil spirit answered them, "Jesus I know, and Paul I know about, but who are you?" Then the man who had the evil spirit jumped on them and overpowered them all. He gave them such a beating that they ran out of the house naked and bleeding. When this became known to the Jews and Greeks living in Ephesus, they were all seized with fear, and the name of the Lord Jesus was held in high honor. Many of those who believed now came and openly confessed what they had done. A number who had practiced sorcery brought their scrolls together and burned them publicly. When they calculated the value of the scrolls,

> the total came to fifty thousand drachmas. In this way the word of the Lord spread widely and grew in power (NIV).

The apostle Paul was very successful in the ministry God had called him to. His ministry was centered on the person and teachings of Jesus Christ. Paul surrendered unconditionally to Jesus Christ despite his privileged position in society. Paul was highly educated and had much authority, but he gave all up to be a servant of Jesus Christ. He considered the kingdom of God first, a sine qua non for successfully working with God.

Paul was diligent, optimistic, and obedient. He was an encourager because he knew that encouragement brings out the best in others. An encourager helps others to grow in the Lord. That is exactly what the apostle Paul was doing—going around to the Churches, teaching, giving his time, helping his brothers and sisters in the Lord, writing letters to them, and showing hospitality to others.

The question is, are you showing any of these traits? Paul lived out the Word of God he was preaching. The apostle Paul knew his life was already secured and ensured for the kingdom of heaven. He made it clear that he was out to win approval, not of people, but of God. He said that if pleasing people had been his goal, he wouldn't have been Christ's servant. Paul admonished the Church to live as citizens of heaven, conducting themselves in a manner worthy of the good news about Christ. Philippians 2:9–14 says,

> Therefore God also has highly exalted Him and given Him the name which is above every name, that at the name of Jesus every knee should bow, of those in heaven, and of those on earth, and of those under the earth, and that every tongue should confess that Jesus Christ is Lord, to the glory of God the Father. Therefore, my beloved, as you have always obeyed, not as in my presence only, but now much more in my absence, work out your own salvation with fear and trembling; for it is God who works

> in you both to will and to do for His good pleasure. Do all things without complaining and disputing (NKJV, emphasis added).

Apostle Paul encourages the Church to confess Jesus Christ as the Lord and Savior because the name of Jesus Christ commands respect and honor to God Almighty alone. Every knee must bow to the name of Jesus Christ either in heaven, on earth, or beneath the earth in humility to honor God. Humility before God should be from a genuine heart. False humility is when the heart of the individual is not humble before God, but on the outside he or she pretends to be humble. Services to God should be genuine, not to impress people but unto the Lord. Eye service can stir up complaints and disputes among brethren, which is not healthy for the Church. The focus of Christians is how they can put in their best in whatever assignment they are given to bring glory to God Almighty.

The apostle Paul was very bold in his ministry because his boldness came from the person of Jesus Christ, whom he'd truly and personally surrendered to. He humbled himself before God, and he was greatly used by God to impact lives, to the glory of God.

Daniel

As a young man, Daniel knew and understood how great and mighty God is. Daniel was among the group of the four young Israelites exiled to Babylon from Jerusalem. Daniel worked with God in obedience and was loyal to His Word, and he became very successful. Daniel refused to be defiled in Babylon because of his belief and faith in God Almighty. Daniel prayed openly, and he refused to worship the gods of that land. He was distinct because of the presence of God in his life.

He was successful because God had given to him an excellent spirit. Through the gift of interpretation of dreams and visions, God lifted Daniel to the second in command in Babylon. The king called Daniel to interpret his dreams. He handled the situation with wisdom and discretion. He sought the face of the Lord that night, and God revealed the secret of the dream to Daniel. Daniel was able to stand before the king with boldness and integrity and to tell the king and the rest of the people in the kingdom who this God is, great and mighty. Daniel 2:14–23, 27–30 says,

> Then Daniel answered with counsel and wisdom to Arioch the captain of the king's guard, which was gone forth to slay the wise men of Babylon: He answered and said to Arioch the king's captain, Why is the decree so hasty from the king? Then Arioch made the thing known to Daniel. Then Daniel went in, and desired of the king that he would give him time, and that he would shew the king the interpretation. Then Daniel went to his house, and made the thing known to Hananiah, Mishael, and Azariah, his companions: That they would desire mercies of the God of heaven concerning this secret; that Daniel and his fellows should not perish with the rest of the wise men of Babylon. Then was the secret revealed unto Daniel in a night vision. Then Daniel blessed the God of heaven. Daniel answered and said, Blessed be the name of God for ever and ever: for wisdom and might are His: And He changeth the times and the seasons: He removeth kings, and setteth up kings: He giveth wisdom unto the wise, and knowledge to them that know understanding: He revealeth the deep and secret things: He knoweth what is in the darkness, and the light dwelleth with Him. I thank thee, and praise thee, O thou God of my fathers, who hast given me wisdom and might, and hast made known unto me now what we desired of thee: for thou hast now made known unto us the king's matter. Daniel answered in the presence of the king, and said, The secret which the king hath demanded cannot the wise men, the astrologers, the magicians, the soothsayers, shew unto the king; But there is a God in heaven that revealeth secrets, and maketh known to the king Nebuchadnezzar what shall be in the latter days. Thy dream, and the visions of thy head upon

thy bed, are these; As for thee, O king, thy thoughts came into thy mind upon thy bed, what should come to pass hereafter: and He that revealeth secrets maketh known to thee what shall come to pass. But as for me, this secret is not revealed to me for any wisdom that I have more than any living, but for their sakes that shall make known the interpretation to the king, and that thou mightest know the thoughts of thy heart (KJV).

Samuel

Samuel was a great man of God and a prophet. The anointing of God was upon Prophet Samuel; that was why he was able to deliver the messages God had given to him without fear and compromise. God was always ministering to Samuel through prophecy to correct, teach, and lead the Israelites and direct them in the right path. Samuel successfully worked with God through his ministry as a prophet because he was obedient and diligent. In 1 Samuel 12:13–24, Samuel said,

> "Now here is the king you have chosen, the one you asked for; see, the Lord has set a king over you. If you fear the Lord and serve and obey Him and do not rebel against His commands, and if both you and the king who reigns over you follow the Lord your God—good! But if you do not obey the Lord, and if you rebel against His commands, His hand will be against you, as it was against your ancestors. Now then, stand still and see this great thing the Lord is about to do before your eyes! Is it not wheat harvest now? I will call on the Lord to send thunder and rain. And you will realize what an evil thing you did in the eyes of the Lord when you asked for a king." Then Samuel called on the Lord, and that same day the Lord sent thunder and rain. So all the people stood in awe of the Lord and of Samuel.
>
> The people all said to Samuel, "Pray to the Lord your God for your servants so that we will not die, for we have added to all our other sins the evil of asking for a king."

"Do not be afraid," Samuel replied. "You have done all this evil; yet do not turn away from the Lord, but serve the Lord with all your heart. Do not turn away after useless idols. They can do you no good, nor can they rescue you, because they are useless. For the sake of His great name the Lord will not reject His people, because the Lord was pleased to make you His own. As for me, far be it from me that I should sin against the Lord by failing to pray for you. And I will teach you the way that is good and right. But be sure to fear the Lord and serve Him faithfully with all your heart; consider what great things He has done for you" (NIV).

2. Fearing the Lord God Almighty

The question is, who is this Lord God Almighty? The Holy Bible, which is the inspirational Word of God and the foundation of Christianity, reveals that God is the Almighty that was not created, because He is the Creator of all things. His handiwork proves to all men that He exists. The Bible says, "Only the fools say in their hearts, "There is no God". They are corrupt, and their actions are evil, not one of them does good!" (Psalms 14:1 NLT) His creation speaks for itself. God is consistent in His Word. God the Father, Son, and the Holy Spirit make up the Trinity. God has the power to change lives no matter how battered they might seem. The Church recognizes Him as the unchangeable God.

God is the ultimate judge, because His decisions are final. That is why man needs to fear Him. His attributes tells us that God is all powerful, sovereign, all knowing, all present, loving, merciful, holy—a righteous judge, and He is a just God. His magnificent characteristics demonstrate to the universe that He is everything we need to live a successful Christian life. Revelations 4:8 says, "Each of the four living creations have six wings and was covered with eyes all around, even under its wings. Day and night they never stop saying, Holy, Holy, Holy, is the Lord God Almighty, who was and is and yet to come" (NIV).

Even the angels recognize the awesomeness of God, who is the true Almighty God, the everlasting, the living God; this is the God the Holy Bible describes and whom I am writing about. Psalm 96 declares the glory of the Lord.

Sing a new song to the Lord!
Let the whole earth sing to the Lord!
Sing to the Lord; praise His Name.
Each day proclaim the good news that He saves.
Publish His glorious deeds among the nations.
Tell everyone about the amazing things He does.
Great is the Lord! He is most worthy of praise!
He is to be feared above all gods.
The gods of other nations are mere idols,
but the Lord made the heavens!
Honor and majesty surround Him;
strength and beauty fills His sanctuary.
O nations of the world, recognize the Lord;
recognize that the Lord is glorious and strong.
Give to the Lord the glory He deserves!
Bring your offering and come into His courts.
Worship the Lord in all His holy splendor.
Let all the earth tremble before Him.
Tell all the nations, "The Lord reigns!"
The world stands firm and cannot be shaken.
He will judge all peoples fairly.
Let the heavens be glad, and the earth rejoice!
Let the sea and everything in it shout His praise!
Let the fields and their crops burst out with joy!
Let the trees of the forest rustle with praise
before the Lord, for He is coming!
He is coming to judge the earth.
He will judge the world with justice,
and the nations with His truth (NLT).

With these attributes of God, the Church has no choice but to fear and revere Him. He is the only one who can destroy both the body and the soul. He is the Creator who was never created and knows our end from the beginning. Matthew 10:28 says, "Don't be afraid of those who want to kill your body; they cannot touch your soul. Fear only God, who can destroy both soul and body in hell" (NLT).

2.1 Revealing Jesus Christ in the Fear of the Lord

Romans 5:1–11 says,

> Therefore, since we have been justified through faith, we have peace with God through our Lord Jesus Christ, through whom we have gained access by faith into this grace in which we now stand. And we boast in the hope of the glory of God. Not only so, but we also glory in our sufferings, because we know that suffering produces perseverance; perseverance, character; and character, hope. And hope does not put us to shame, because God's love has been poured out into our hearts through the Holy Spirit, who has been given to us. You see, at just the right time, when we were still powerless, Christ died for the ungodly. Very rarely will anyone die for a righteous person, though for a good person someone might possibly dare to die. But God demonstrates His own love for us in this: While we were still sinners, Christ died for us. Since we have now been justified by His blood, how much more shall we be saved from God's wrath through Him! For if, while we were God's enemies, we were reconciled to Him through the death of His Son, how much more, having been reconciled, shall we be saved through His life! Not only is this so, but we also boast in God through our Lord Jesus Christ, through whom we have now received reconciliation (NIV).

The salvation God gave us wasn't earned by any individual work. It is by His grace and mercy that God sent His only begotten Son to reconcile us to Himself after man fell from His grace. Knowing His Son, Jesus Christ, is the only sure way to know the fear of the Lord and the selfless love contained in fearing God.

The love of God is demonstrated in His Word and in the finished work of our Lord Jesus Christ, which is boldly and clearly written in the Holy Bible. God is a loving Father, and on the other hand, He is very slow to anger.

2.2The "Truth, "asRevealedtotheChurch, IsJesusChrist

Through the Person of Jesus Christ, the Church experience God's Grace. God has empowered the Church with His grace to live life to the fullest only by the power of the Holy Spirit. A Christian can only experience it, through obedience to the Word of God, to be successful in his or her walk with God. Matthew 16:15–19 says,

> Then He asked them, "But who do you say I am?" Simon Peter answered, "You are the Messiah, the Son of the living God." Jesus replied, "You are blessed, Simon son of John, because my Father in heaven has revealed this to you. You did not learn this from any human being. Now I say to you that you are Peter (which means 'rock'), and upon this rock I will build my church, and all the powers of hell will not conquer it. And I will give you the keys of the Kingdom of Heaven. Whatever you forbid on earth will be forbidden in heaven, and whatever you permit on earth will be permitted in heaven" (NLT).

The above statement by Jesus Christ laid the foundation for Christianity. The additional assurances in the above statement provide a basis for a Christian to be successful. Jesus Christ has given the Church the spiritual keys to be successful. Ephesians 6:10–18 says,

> A final word: Be strong in the Lord and in His mighty power. Put on all of God's armor so that you will be able to stand firm against all strategies of the devil. For we are not fighting against flesh-and-blood enemies, but against evil rulers and authorities of the unseen world, against

> mighty powers in this dark world, and against evil spirits in the heavenly places. Therefore, put on every piece of God's armor so you will be able to resist the enemy in the time of evil. Then after the battle you will still be standing firm. Stand your ground, putting on the belt of truth and the body armor of God's righteousness. For shoes, put on the peace that comes from the Good News so that you will be fully prepared. In addition to all of these, hold up the shield of faith to stop the fiery arrows of the devil. Put on salvation as your helmet, and take the sword of the Spirit, which is the word of God. Pray in the Spirit at all times and on every occasion. Stay alert and be persistent in your prayers for all believers everywhere (NLT).

The true foundation can come only from the fear of the Lord God Almighty. Living a successful Christian life is built on only the wisdom of God from His Word. Truly that individual will be successful both spiritually and physically. Proverbs 9:10–11 says, "The fear of the Lord is the beginning of wisdom, and knowledge of the Holy One is understanding. For through wisdom your days will be many, and years will be added to your life" (NIV).

3. Living for God by His Word

The various passages of the scriptures listed below should remind the Church on how we should live for God by His Word through our actions.

Malachi 1:12–13 says, "But you dishonor my name with your actions. By bringing contemptible food, you are saying it's all right to defile the Lord's Table. You say, 'It's too hard to serve the Lord,' and you turn up your noses at my commands,' says the Lord of Heaven's Armies. 'Think of it! Animals that are stolen and crippled and sick are being presented as offerings! Should I accept from you such offerings as these?' asks the Lord."

The Bible says, "Honor God with your wealth and with the best part of everything you produce" (Proverbs 3:9 NLT).

The book of Malachi is telling the Church that offerings presented to God should come from the best of our possessions or wealth with a cheerful heart. The Lord detests honor that is tainted or halfhearted. The manner in which the Church gives offerings to God is very important to Him. He sees every aspect of how the Church presents tithes and offerings, to know if the Church is truly faithful to Him. The act of "selfless giving" is often difficult, especially when there is no immediate return. This is particularly so if the individual has not totally surrendered that part of his or her life and does not live for God. God is self-sufficient; gold and silver belong to Him. When the Church gives sincerely to the services of His work, God turns it around to be a blessing to that individual. God is not in need of anything.

God wants His Church to be faithful to Him with its finances. He gave the Church everything to live a successful Christian life. To live for God is to trust Him with our resources because He is the giver. The Church is encouraged to give willingly and not grudgingly. The tithes and offerings to God must come from a genuine source of an income, not stolen property or something without value. The Word of God discourages stolen property to be given to Him. God must be respected with the tithes and offerings we offer to Him.

Matthew 22:37–40 says, "Jesus replied, 'You must love the Lord your God with all your heart, all your soul, and all your mind.' This is the first and greatest commandment. A second is equally important: 'Love your neighbor as yourself.' The entire law and all the demands of the prophets are based on these two commandments" (NLT).

The book of Matthew is encouraging the Church to live for God in the way we love. To live a successful Christian life, we must love God with all our heart, soul, and mind, and also love our neighbors as ourselves. The love of God should flow from sincere hearts not from the lips alone.

Ephesians 5:1–10 says,

> Imitate God, therefore, in everything you do, because you are His dear children. Live a life filled with love, following the example of Christ. He loved us and offered Himself as a sacrifice for us, a pleasing aroma to God. Let there be no sexual immorality, impurity, or greed among you. Such sins have no place among God's people. Obscene stories, foolish talk, and coarse jokes—these are not for you. Instead, let there be thankfulness to God. You can be sure that no immoral, impure, or greedy person will inherit the Kingdom of Christ and of God. For a greedy person is an idolater, worshiping the things of this world. Don't be fooled by those who try to excuse these sins, for the anger of God will fall on all who disobey Him. Don't participate in the things these people do. For once you

> were full of darkness, but now you have light from the Lord. So live as people of light! For this light within you produces only what is good and right and true. Carefully determine what pleases the Lord (NLT).

The book of Ephesians is also telling the Church to live by His Word to imitate God in everything a Christian does. The Church should be the light that draws the ungodly to God by the way its members live. The Church should not copy the lifestyle of the ungodly, but rather, the ungodly should be attracted to our lifestyle by the way we live for God.

First Peter 2:1–10 says,

> So get rid of all evil behavior. Be done with all deceit, hypocrisy, jealousy, and all unkind speech. Like newborn babies, you must crave pure spiritual milk so that you will grow into a full experience of salvation. Cry out for this nourishment, now that you have had a taste of the Lord's kindness. You are coming to Christ, who is the living cornerstone of God's temple. He was rejected by people, but He was chosen by God for great honor. And you are living stones that God is building into His spiritual temple. What's more, you are His holy priests. Through the mediation of Jesus Christ, you offer spiritual sacrifices that please God. As the Scriptures say, "I am placing a cornerstone in Jerusalem, chosen for great honor, and anyone who trusts in Him will never be disgraced." Yes, you who trust Him recognize the honor God has given Him. But for those who reject Him, "The stone that the builders rejected has now become the cornerstone." And, "He is the stone that makes people stumble, the rock that makes them fall." They stumble because they do not obey God's word, and so they meet the fate that was planned for them. But you are not like that, for you are a chosen people. You are royal priests, a holy nation, and God's very own possession. As a result, you can show others the

> goodness of God, for He called you out of the darkness into His wonderful light. "Once you had no identity as a people; now you are God's people. Once you received no mercy; now you have received God's mercy" (NLT).

Peter is encouraging the Church to crave pure spiritual milk, which is the Word of God. The Word of God will help the Church to mature fully in its walk with God to live for Him. The Church is instructed to get rid of evil behavior, because that will hinder spiritual nourishment and growth in the fullness of Christ. Peter made it clear to the Church that, on our own, we can't have an identity; but it is only in Christ that we have an identity. The Church should be identified as followers of Christ. As children of God, we will live for God by His Word to shine out the light of God even in this dark world.

Galatians 5:16–26 says,

> So I say, let the Holy Spirit guide your lives. Then you won't be doing what your sinful nature craves. The sinful nature wants to do evil, which is just the opposite of what the Spirit wants. And the Spirit gives us desires that are the opposite of what the sinful nature desires. These two forces are constantly fighting each other, so you are not free to carry out your good intentions. But when you are directed by the Spirit, you are not under obligation to the Law of Moses. When you follow the desires of your sinful nature, the results are very clear: sexual immorality, impurity, lustful pleasures, idolatry, sorcery, hostility, quarreling, jealousy, outbursts of anger, selfish ambition, dissension, division, envy, drunkenness, wild parties, and other sins like these. Let me tell you again, as I have before, that anyone living that sort of life will not inherit the Kingdom of God. But the Holy Spirit produces this kind of fruit in our lives: love, joy, peace, patience, kindness, goodness, faithfulness, gentleness, and self-control.

> There is no law against these things! Those who belong to Christ Jesus have nailed the passions and desires of their sinful nature to His cross and crucified them there. Since we are living by the Spirit, let us follow the Spirit's leading in every part of our lives. Let us not become conceited, or provoke one another, or be jealous of one another (NLT).

Apostle Paul's writings to the Galatians serves to remind the Church today that there are two forces constantly at war in the life of a Christian: the sinful nature, which is evil and opposite the Word of God, and the Holy Spirit, which enables a Christian to live for God. The force that controls a Christian determines if the individual truly lives for God by His Word. The sinful nature can only be disciplined by the power of the Holy Spirit when a Christian lives for God by His Word. The sinful nature can only be subdued when a Christian is filled with the Holy Spirit. The sinful nature leads to the desires of the flesh, which is very destructive to the life of that individual because it leads to sin, which will prevent the individual from inheriting the kingdom of God. There is an opportunity for the individual to repent; God will forgive you. The Church is encouraged to seek the guidance of the Holy Spirit to live for God by His Word.

Ephesians 5:15–20 says, "So be careful how you live. Don't live like fools, but like those who are wise. Make the most of every opportunity in these evil days. Don't act thoughtlessly, but understand what the Lord wants you to do. Don't be drunk with wine, because that will ruin your life. Instead, be filled with the Holy Spirit, singing psalms and hymns and spiritual songs among yourselves, and making music to the Lord in your hearts. And give thanks for everything to God the Father in the name of our Lord Jesus Christ (NLT).

The importance of the Holy Spirit in the life of a Christian cannot be overemphasized. Apostle Paul is encouraging the

Church not to be "drunk with wine" but to be filled with the Holy Spirit so that the Christian can live for God by His Word. When a person is drunk with wine, the resulting intoxication produces evil work, while the Holy Spirit energizes a Christian to produce good work to glorify God.

4. Fear God

To fear is to have reverential awe of God, to be afraid or apprehensive. Living a successful Christian life requires total obedience to the will of God and means having reverential awe of God. The grace of God to forgive sin isn't taken for granted; fear God in the open and in secret.

These are ways scripture describes how we should fear God, and they are as follows:

Deuteronomy 6:13 says, "You must fear the Lord your God and serve Him. When you take an oath, you must use only His name" (NLT).

Deuteronomy 8:6 says, "So obey the commands of the Lord your God by walking in His ways and fearing Him" (NLT).

Deuteronomy 13:4 says, "Serve only the Lord your God and fear Him alone. Obey His commands, listen to His voice, and cling to Him" (NLT).

Deuteronomy 31:12 says, "Call them all together—men, women, children, and the foreigners living in your towns—so they may hear this book of instruction and learn to fear the Lord your God and carefully obey all the terms of these instructions" (NLT).

Joshua 4:24 says, "He did this so all the nations of the earth might know that the Lord's hand is powerful, and so you might fear the Lord your God forever" (NLT).

First Samuel 12:14 says, "Now if you fear and worship the Lord and listen to His voice, and if you do not rebel against the

Lord's commands, then both you and your king will show that you recognize the Lord as your God" (NLT).

Nehemiah 5:15 says, "The former governors, in contrast, had laid heavy burdens on the people, demanding a daily ration of food and wine, besides forty pieces of silver. Even their assistants took advantage of the people. But because I feared God, I did not act that way" (NLT).

Nehemiah 7:2 says, "I gave the responsibilities of governing Jerusalem to my brother Hanani along with Hananiah, the commander of the fortress, for he was a faithful man, who feared God more than most" (NLT).

Psalm 34:7 says, "For the angel of the Lord is a guard; he surrounds and defends all who fear him" (NLT).

Psalm 61:5 says, "For you have heard my vows, O God. You have given me an inheritance reserved for those who fear your name" (NLT).

Psalm 76:7 says, "No wonder you are greatly feared! Who can stand before you when your anger explodes?" (NLT).

Psalm 103:17 says, "But the love of the Lord remains forever with those who fear Him. His salvation extends to the children's children" (NLT).

Psalm 128:1 says, "How joyful are those who fear the Lord—all who follows His ways!" (NLT).

Proverbs 8:13 says, "All who fear the Lord will hate evil. Therefore, I hate pride and arrogance, corruption and perverse speech" (NLT).

Proverbs 28:14 says, "Blessed are those who fear to do wrong, but the stubborn are headed for serious trouble" (NLT).

Proverbs 31:30 says, "Charm is deceptive, and beauty does not last; but a woman who fears the Lord will be greatly praised" (NLT).

Isaiah 25:3 says, "Therefore, strong nations will declare your glory; ruthless nations will fear you" (NLT).

Jeremiah 2:19 says, "Your wickedness will bring its own punishment. Your turning from me will shame you. You will see what an evil, bitter thing it is to abandon the Lord your God and not to fear Him. I, the Lord, the Lord of Heaven's Armies, have spoken!" (NLT).

Malachi 3:16 says, "Then those who feared the Lord spoke with each other, and the Lord listened to what they said. In His presence, a scroll of remembrance was written to record the names of those who feared Him and always thought about the honor of His name" (NLT).

Malachi 4:2 says, "But for you who fear my name, the Son of righteousness will rise healings in His Wings. And you will go free, leaping with joy like calves let out to pasture" (NLT).

Second Corinthians 7:1 says, "Because we have those promises, dear friends, let us cleanse ourselves from everything that can defile our body or spirit. And let's work toward complete holiness because we fear God" (NLT).

Revelation 11:17–18 says, "And they said, 'We give thanks to you, Lord God, the Almighty, the one who is and who always was, for now you have assumed your great power and have begun to reign. The nations were filled with wrath, but now the time of your wrath has come. It is time to judge the dead and reward your servants the prophets, as well as your holy people, and all who fear your name, from the least to the greatest. It is time to destroy all who caused destruction on the earth'" (NLT).

First Thessalonians 4:7–9 says, "God has called us to live holy lives, not impure lives. Therefore, anyone who refuses to live by these rules is not disobeying human teaching but is rejecting God, who gives His Holy Spirit to you. But we don't need to write to you about the importance of loving each other, for God Himself has taught you to love one another" (NLT).

First John 4:7–21 says,

> Dear friends, let us continue to love one another, for love comes from God. Anyone who loves is a child of God and knows God. But anyone who does not love does not know God, for God is love. God showed how much He loved us by sending His one and only Son into the world so that we might have eternal life through Him. This is

> real love—not that we loved God, but that He loved us and sent His Son as a sacrifice to take away our sins. Dear friends, since God loved us that much, we surely ought to love each other. No one has ever seen God. But if we love each other, God lives in us, and His love is brought to full expression in us. And God has given us His Spirit as proof that we live in Him and He in us. Furthermore, we have seen with our own eyes and now testify that the Father sent His Son to be the Savior of the world. All who confess that Jesus is the Son of God have God living in them, and they live in God. We know how much God loves us, and we have put our trust in His love. God is love, and all who live in love live in God, and God lives in them. And as we live in God, our love grows more perfect. So we will not be afraid on the Day of Judgment, but we can face Him with confidence because we live like Jesus here in this world. Such love has no fear, because perfect love expels all fear. If we are afraid, it is for fear of punishment, and this shows that we have not fully experienced His perfect love. We love each other because He loved us first. If someone says, "I love God," but hates a Christian brother or sister, that person is a liar; for if we don't love people we can see, how can we love God, whom we cannot see? And He has given us this command: Those who love God must also love their fellow believers (NLT).

Psalm 51:16–17 says, "You do not desire a sacrifice, or I would offer one. You do not want a burnt offering. The sacrifice you desire is a broken spirit. You will not reject a broken and repentant heart, O God" (NLT).

5. Know the Lord Jesus Christ

Any individual who knows the Lord Jesus Christ truly understands the Word of God. Jesus Christ is the Church's righteousness. The Church is encouraged to seek God through His Word. Jesus Christ is the true representative of who God is. Jesus Christ is the Word who dwells among men. He is the Savior, Bright Morning Star, Alpha and the Omega, Advocate, Counselor, Redeemer, Encourager, and Comforter. Jesus Christ promised the Church the Holy Spirit, who is the Comforter, as He was ascending to heaven. Knowing Jesus Christ means to understand the Word of God. It is impossible to be successful in the Christian walk without knowing the person of Jesus Christ. Knowing and adopting the leadership example of Jesus Christ will make a Christian more effective and productive while being successful. Jesus Christ is our standard because He set the pace.

John 1:1–17 says,

> In the beginning was the Word, and the Word was with God, and the Word was God. He was with God in the beginning. Through Him all things were made; without Him nothing was made that has been made. In Him was life, and that life was the light of all mankind. The light shines in the darkness, and the darkness has not overcome it. There was a man sent from God whose name was John. He came as a witness to testify concerning that light, so that through him all might believe. He himself

> was not the light; he came only as a witness to the light. The true light that gives light to everyone was coming into the world. He was in the world, and though the world was made through Him, the world did not recognize Him. He came to that which was His own, but His own did not receive Him. Yet to all who did receive Him, to those who believed in His name, He gave the right to become children of God—children born not of natural descent, nor of human decision or a husband's will, but born of God. The Word became flesh and made His dwelling among us. We have seen His glory, the glory of the one and only Son, who came from the Father, full of grace and truth. (John testified concerning Him. He cried out, saying, "This is the one I spoke about when I said, 'He who comes after me has surpassed me because He was before me.'") Out of His fullness we have all received grace in place of grace already given. For the law was given through Moses; grace and truth came through Jesus Christ (NIV).

Those who received Jesus Christ as their Lord and Savior, God gave the right to become children of God. Jesus Christ existed with God right from the creation of time. He is the Word of God and the light to the world. Jesus Christ, who was born of God, became flesh to reveal God the Father through Him. John was sent to witness and testify about the true light, who is Jesus Christ, that through Him people will be saved from their sins. Grace was given to man, through Jesus Christ by God. If anyone repents and comes to God, the individual will be justified because of Jesus Christ. Jesus Christ is God in the flesh. Colossians 1:15 says, "Christ is the visible image of the invisible God. He existed before anything was created and is supreme over all creation" (NLT). What make a believer successful is knowing and accepting Jesus Christ as Lord and personal Savior, knowing who he or she is in Christ, and doing what pleases God. Our anchor is in Jesus Christ, who is the author and the finisher of our faith. He has given us the authority of His Word to equip His Church.

God's Word leads the Christian to succeed. Knowing His Word is essential for a believer to grow spiritually and physically. "Your word is a lamp to guide my feet and a light for my path" (Psalm 119:105 NLT).

It is true that without light we can easily stumble in the dark, but with light we can easily navigate to anywhere. The Word of God is the lamp for the Church to see clearly both in the physical and the spiritual worlds. To be overcomers, the Word of God should be strong and rooted in us—in body, soul, and mind. Even when we are sleeping, the Word of God will be alive in us. Jesus Christ showed us an example when the devil tempted Him. He quoted from the scripture.

The Word of God is the source from where we derive our daily wisdom, knowledge, and strength to succeed in this evil world, because that is what the devil bows to and trembles with fear. Our Lord Jesus gave us an example when He was tempted; He used the Word as a weapon against the devil. Jesus Christ resisted the devil's deception with the Word. Jesus Christ is God. He demonstrated it to show us how we as believers can succeed and defeat the devil by the Word of God. The temptation of Jesus Christ exposes some of the devil's devices, which he uses to lure many away from the faith if they are not grounded in the Word of God. Which voice are you hearing today? The voice of God will not mislead the Christian who diligently and daily seeks the face of God through His Word.

Matthew 4:3–11 says,

> During that time the devil came and said to Him, "If you are the Son of God, tell these stones to become loaves of bread."
>
> But Jesus told him, "No! The Scriptures say, 'People do not live by bread alone, but by every word that comes from the mouth of God.'"
>
> Then the devil took Him to the holy city, Jerusalem, to the highest point of the Temple, and said, "If you are the Son of God, jump off! For the Scriptures say, 'He will

> order His angels to protect you. And they will hold you up with their hands so you won't even hurt your foot on a stone.'"
>
> Jesus responded, "The Scriptures also say, 'You must not test the Lord your God.'"
>
> Next the devil took Him to the peak of a very high mountain and showed Him all the kingdoms of the world and their glory. "I will give it all to you," he said, "if you will kneel down and worship me."
>
> "Get out of here, Satan," Jesus told him. "For the Scriptures say, 'You must worship the Lord your God and serve only Him.'" Then the devil went away, and angels came and took care of Jesus (NLT).

Jesus Christ clearly showed us how to be successful through the Word of God. Living out the Word is essential. Quoting the Bible and obeying it are two separate actions. Christians who study the Word of God, meditate on it, and believe on the Word of God as given will live to exhibit trust in God in their daily lives. They will also know Jesus Christ personally, and their lives will be a living testimony to the glory of God.

Romans 15:13 says, "I pray that God, the source of hope, will fill you completely with joy and peace because you trust in Him. Then you will overflow with confident hope through the power of the Holy Spirit" (NLT).

Luke 6:46–49 says,

> So why do you keep calling me "Lord, Lord!" when you don't do what I say? I will show you what it's like when someone comes to me, listens to my teaching, and then follows it. It is like a person building a house who digs deep and lays the foundation on solid rock. When the floodwaters rise and break against that house, it stands firm because it is well built. But anyone who hears and doesn't obey is like a person who builds a house without a foundation. When the floods sweep down against that house, it will collapse into a heap of ruins (NLT).

Any relationship built on lies is a relationship on a faulty foundation. The one-and-only way to have a solid foundation is by building our faith on the knowledge of Jesus Christ through His Word and by practicing it by the power of the Holy Spirit.

James 1:22–25 says, "But don't just listen to God's word. You must do what it says. Otherwise, you are only fooling yourselves. For if you listen to the word and don't obey, it is like glancing at your face in a mirror. You see yourself, walk away, and forget what you look like. But if you look carefully into the perfect law that sets you free, and if you do what it says and don't forget what you heard, then God will bless you for doing it" (NLT).

The Word of God is our daily mirror, which successful Christians glance at to manage their day. Doing the will of God comes with blessings. Challenges will come, but God will turn all the challenges to successes.

First Peter 1:3–5, 15 says,

> All praise to God, the Father of our Lord Jesus Christ. It is by His great mercy that we have been born again, because God raised Jesus Christ from the dead. Now we live with great expectation, and we have a priceless inheritance—an inheritance that is kept in heaven for you, pure and undefiled, beyond the reach of change and decay. And through your faith, God is protecting you by His power until you receive this salvation, which is ready to be revealed on the last day for all to see…But now you must be holy in everything you do, just as God who chose you is holy (NLT).

The Word is a spoken word from God, and it comes with power. It is the living proof of God. Deuteronomy 11:18–19 says, "So commit yourselves wholeheartedly to these words of mine. Tie them to your hands and wear them on your forehead as reminders. Teach them to your children. Talk about them when you are at home and when you are on the road, when you are going to bed and when you are getting up" (NLT).

Ephesians 5:31–32 says, "As the Scriptures say, 'A man leaves his father and mother and is joined to his wife, and the two are united into one.' This is a great mystery, but it is an illustration of the way Christ and the Church are one" (NLT).

Second Thessalonians 3:3 says, "But the Lord is faithful; He will strengthen you and guard you from the evil one" (NLT). Knowing the Lord Jesus Christ gives assurance of safety and peace that the world cannot give. He is faithful to His Word and will never leave His flock unattended. The evil one will roar, but the safety net provided by the Lord will guarantee a successful Christian life, if Christians remain within the confines of the safety net of Christ.

Hebrews 6:17–19 says, "God also bound himself with an oath, so that those who received the promise could be perfectly sure that He would never change His mind. So God has given both His promise and His oath. These two things are unchangeable because it is impossible for God to lie. Therefore, we who have fled to Him for refuge can have great confidence as we hold to the hope that lies before us. This hope is a strong and trustworthy anchor for our souls. It leads us through the curtain into God's inner sanctuary" (NLT).

Hebrews 10:19–24 says,

> And so, dear brothers and sisters, we can boldly enter heaven's Most Holy Place because of the blood of Jesus. By His death, Jesus opened a new and life-giving way through the curtain into the Most Holy Place. And since we have a great High Priest who rules over God's house, let us go right into the presence of God with sincere hearts fully trusting Him. For our guilty consciences have been sprinkled with Christ's blood to make us clean, and our bodies have been washed with pure water. Let us hold tightly without wavering to the hope we affirm, for God can be trusted to keep His promise. Let us think of ways to motivate one another to acts of love and good works (NLT).

First John 5:1 says, "Everyone who believes that Jesus is the Christ has become a child of God. And everyone who loves the Father loves His children, too" (NLT).

Jude 1:17–24 says,

> But you, my dear friends, must remember what the apostles of our Lord Jesus Christ said. They told you that in the last times there would be scoffers whose purpose in life is to satisfy their ungodly desires. These people are the ones who are creating divisions among you. They follow their natural instincts because they do not have God's Spirit in them. But you, dear friends, must build each other up in your most holy faith, pray in the power of the Holy Spirit, and await the mercy of our Lord Jesus Christ, who will bring you eternal life. In this way, you will keep yourselves safe in God's love. And you must show mercy to those whose faith is wavering. Rescue others by snatching them from the flames of judgment. Show mercy to still others, but do so with great caution, hating the sins that contaminate their lives. Now all glory to God, who is able to keep you from falling away and will bring you with great joy into His glorious presence without a single fault (NLT).

6. Honor Your Father and Mother

Exodus 20:12 says, "Honor your father and mother. Then you will live a long, full life in the land the Lord your God is giving you" (NLT). God's desire for the Church is that His Word should be honored and treated with respect. God started building His Church from the family. Orderliness in the Church can start only when a family is under the leadership of God Almighty. God is calling the Church for true change and repentance in regard to how parents and older people are to be treated at home and in the Church. The Bible makes it clear that those in the Church should teach and practice respect for one another.

Family is what God ordained from the beginning of His creation. God commanded that children should obey their parents so they can be successful. God's will is that the Church should be an example of living out the Word of God to respect and honor elders and those who are old enough to be parents. To neglect elderly parents is against the will of God. Education or riches doesn't give a child the right to disrespect his or her parent. First Timothy 5:1–2 says, "Do not rebuke an older man harshly, but exhort him as if he were your father. Treat younger men as brothers, older women as mothers, and younger women as sisters, with absolute purity" (NIV).

God impressed in my heart that the reason some Christians are working so hard today without making progress is because of disrespect and dishonor for their parents sometime in their lives without their repentance. Are you in the category of children whom their parents abandoned, abused, or provoked? The Lord wants you to forgive and reconcile with them, so it will be well with you to live a successful Christian life. Matthew 6:14–15 says, "If you forgive those who sin against you your heavenly Father will forgive you. But if you refuse to forgive others, your Father will not forgive your sins" (NLT). To be successful in your Christian walk, forgiveness must be part of your daily lifestyle. The Church is encouraged to forgive because God forgave us. Forgiveness is one of the keys to success.

Christians are strongly encouraged to routinely carry out soul searching, and if they discover that they have fallen short of this command, they should go without delay to apologize and reconcile with their parents so that it will be well with them to live a successful Christian life. If your parents are no more or are unreachable, earnestly seek the face of God, and ask for forgiveness so that "it will be well with you."

Ephesians 6:1–4 says, "Children, obey your parents because you belong to the Lord, for this is the right thing to do. 'Honor your father and mother.' This is the first commandment with a promise: If you honor your father and mother, 'things will go well for you, and you will have a long life on the earth.' Fathers, do not provoke your children to anger by the way you treat them. Rather, bring them up with the discipline and instruction that comes from the Lord" (NLT).

Second Timothy 3:1–5, 8 says,

> You should know this, Timothy, that in the last days there will be very difficult times. For people will love only themselves and their money. They will be boastful and proud, scoffing at God, *disobedient to their parents, and ungrateful.* They will consider nothing sacred. They will be unloving and unforgiving; they will slander others and have no self-control. They will be cruel and hate what is good. They will betray their friends, be reckless, be puffed up with

> pride, and love pleasure rather than God. *They will act religious, but they will reject the power that could make them godly.* Stay away from people like that! These teachers oppose the truth just as Jannes and Jambres opposed Moses. *They have depraved minds and a counterfeit faith* (NIV, emphasis added).

This passage was the advice from the apostle Paul to Timothy about difficult times in the last days. Apostle Paul admonished his "son" Timothy to stay away from false teachers who oppose the true Word of God to live for themselves. They have depraved minds and counterfeit faith, and Timothy was advised to beware of these sorts of people who go against the Word of God by the way they behave. These sorts of people will not consider anything holy. They will love themselves and money, be boastful and proud, be unloving and unforgiving, hate what is good, and be disobedient to their parents. These kind of children will act so religious but reject the power of the Word of God that will make them able to live a holy life. To live fulfilling and satisfying lives, children must obey God by His Word. This advice does apply to the Church of today. Our world today has become inundated with practices and news about these same things that the apostle Paul wrote about thousands of years ago. God has adopted us, through Christ, to do something through the way we live our lives and positively influence the world.

Proverbs 3:1–6 says,

> My child, never forget the things I have taught you. Store my commands in your heart. If you do this, you will live many years, and your life will be satisfying. Never let loyalty and kindness leave you! Tie them around your neck as a reminder. Write them deep within your heart. Then you will find favor with both God and people, and you will earn a good reputation. Trust in the Lord with all your heart; do not depend on your own understanding. Seek

His will in all you do, and He will show you which path to take (NLT).

Matthew 15:3–9 says,

> Jesus replied, "And why do you break the command of God for the sake of your tradition? For God said, 'Honor your father and mother' and 'anyone who curses their father or mother is to be put to death.' But you say that if anyone declares that what might have been used to help their father or mother is 'devoted to God,' they are not to 'honor their father or mother' with it. Thus you nullify the word of God for the sake of your tradition. You hypocrites! Isaiah was right when he prophesied about you: 'These people honor me with their lips, but their hearts are far from me. They worship me in vain; their teachings are merely human rules'" (NIV).

Respect and honor for God and parents must be genuine and total. Children that refuse to honor their parents face difficulties because they disobey God's command. This is one commandment of God that is with a promise, and, therefore, occupies a special place in the heart of God. The traditions in the society should not contradict the Word of God in our lives to respect our parents or the elderly. The tradition of God is laid out in the Word of God to be respectful to parents; that is why the body of Christ is unique and different. Any child that rebels against godly advice from parents is going in a wrong direction. Rebellion is a sin in the sight of God. First Samuel 15:23a says, "Rebellion is as sinful as witchcraft, and stubbornness as bad as worshiping Idols" (NLT). God wants His Church to honor Him with His Word by honoring our parents and the elders. Children should honor their parents weather they are young or old. For this reason some parents lament every day because of disrespect and lack of care from their children. Their parents go through pain, not because of their circumstances but for the fact that their children have rebelled and abandon them. Some children have deliberately refused to take care of their parents even in their old age. The Church is admonished today by the Word of God to repent from such acts of rebellion and disrespect to parents and elders. I encourage the Church to honor God with heart, mind, soul, and strength through obeying His Word; it will make a great difference in the body of Christ. The Holy Bible says that the instructions of God are the key to life.

Proverbs 4:10–13 says, "My child, listen to me and do as I say, and you will have a long, good life. I will teach you wisdom's ways and lead you in straight paths. When you walk, you won't be held back; when you run, you won't stumble. Take hold of my instructions; don't let them go. Guard them, for they are the key to life (NLT).

Epilogue

Jesus Christ is calling His Church today for true repentance and total cleansing from every kind of sin in order to be successful in the Christian walk. Jesus Christ is standing at the door of your heart today, and He is knocking. It is your decision to open your heart to Him or not. The Church is encouraged today to rethink and make amends with the Lord from where the Church has fallen. It is possible to live a successful Christian life by His grace. When a Christian is spiritually guided with the Word of God, it helps the Christian to establish a strong relationship with God. The relationship can only be established when the individual meditates on the Word of God daily in his or her heart and walks in accordance with His Word.

Lies and deception have gradually gained a foothold into the Church. God is telling His Church today to repent from it. The Church should run away from evil because sin is a barrier between the Church and God. This barrier can only be broken by true repentance and total surrender to God. Revelation 21:8 says, "But cowards, unbelievers, the corrupt, murderers, the immoral, those who practice witchcraft, idol worshippers, and all liars—their fate is in the fiery lake of burning sulfur. This is the second death" (NLT).

The Church needs thorough self-examination. God gave His Word to correct His Church to live a successful Christian life. The Lord rebukes those who He loves according to the Holy Bible. Revelation 3:19–22 says, "Those whom I love I rebuke and discipline. So be earnest and repent. Here I am! I stand at the door and knock. If anyone hears my voice and opens the door, I will come in and eat with that person, and they with me. To the one who is victorious, I will give the right to sit with me on my throne, just as I was victorious and sat down with my Father on His throne. Whoever has ears, let them hear what the Spirit say to the churches" (NIV).

Romans 2:4–29 says,

> Don't you see how wonderfully kind, tolerant, and patient God is with you? Does this mean nothing to you? Can't you see that His kindness is intended to turn you from your sin? But because you are stubborn and refuse to turn from your sin, you are storing up terrible punishment for yourself. For a day of anger is coming, when God's righteous judgment will be revealed. He will judge everyone according to what they have done. He will give eternal life to those who keep on doing good, seeking after the glory and honor and immortality that God offers. But He will pour out His anger and wrath on those who live for themselves, who refuse to obey the truth and instead live lives of wickedness. There will be trouble and calamity for everyone who keeps on doing what is evil—for the Jew first and also for the Gentile. But there will be glory and honor and peace from God for all who do good—for the Jew first and also for the Gentile. For God does not show favoritism. When the Gentiles sin, they will be destroyed, even though they never had God's written law. And the Jews, who do have God's law, will be judged by that law when they fail to obey it. For merely listening to the law doesn't make us right with God. It is obeying the law that makes us right in His sight. Even Gentiles, who do not have God's written law, show that they know His law when they instinctively obey it, even without having heard it. They demonstrate that God's law is written in their hearts, for their own conscience and thoughts either accuse them or tell them they are doing right. And this is the message

> I proclaim—that the day is coming when God, through Christ Jesus, will judge everyone's secret life. You who call yourselves Jews are relying on God's law, and you boast about your special relationship with Him. You know what He wants; you know what is right because you have been taught His law. You are convinced that you are a guide for the blind and a light for people who are lost in darkness. You think you can instruct the ignorant and teach children the ways of God. For you are certain that God's law gives you complete knowledge and truth. Well then, if you teach others, why don't you teach yourself? You tell others not to steal, but do you steal? You say it is wrong to commit adultery, but do you commit adultery? You condemn idolatry, but do you use items stolen from pagan temples? You are so proud of knowing the law, but you dishonor God by breaking it. No wonder the Scriptures say, "The Gentiles blaspheme the name of God because of you." The Jewish ceremony of circumcision has value only if you obey God's law. But if you don't obey God's law, you are no better off than an uncircumcised Gentile. And if the Gentiles obey God's law, won't God declare them to be His own people? In fact, uncircumcised Gentiles who keep God's law will condemn you Jews who are circumcised and possess God's law but don't obey it. For you are not a true Jew just because you were born of Jewish parents or because you have gone through the ceremony of circumcision. No, a true Jew is one whose heart is right with God. And true circumcision is not merely obeying the letter of the law; rather, it is a change of heart produced by the Spirit. And a person with a changed heart seeks praise from God, not from people" (NLT).

God has given His Word to the Church very boldly and clearly for the Church to live by in the Holy Bible. The truth is that the spiritual sustainer of a Christian is the Word of God alone, in obedience to Him, to live a successful Christian life.

As you read this book, if you have not received the Lord Jesus Christ as your Lord and personal Savior, you are invited to receive His free gift of salvation. He is ready to forgive you to live a new life and be successful.

Notes

Notes

38330334R00059

Made in the USA
Charleston, SC
05 February 2015